PALO MAYOMBE

SPIRITS - RITUALS - SPELLS
THE DARKSIDE OF SANTERIA

CARLOS GALDIANO MONTENEGRO

ORIGINAL PUBLICATIONS
PLAINVIEW, NEW YORK

DEDICATION

This book is dedicated to El Cristo Negro, my Ancestor Spirits and to the Spirits of Palo Mayombe whom have been my guides in a world of colored darkness.

Carlos Galdiano Montenegro

PALO MAYOMBE

SPIRITS - RITUALS - SPELLS

ISBN: 0-942272-41-2

**COPYRIGHT (C) 1994 CARLOS MONTENEGRO
ALL RIGHTS RESERVED**

For a complete catalog of over 450 titles send $2.00 to:

ORIGINAL PUBLICATIONS
P.O. Box 236
Old Bethpage, New York 11804-0236

No part of this book may be reproduced in any manner without written permission from the publisher. This book contains formulas that were used in the historical practice of Palo Mayombe in Cuba, Puerto Rico, and Brazil. Currently, there are strict guidelines and restrictions in the use of and or buying and selling of human bones in the United States. This book also contains elements of animal sacrifice which is historically a part of the Santeria and Palo Mayombe Religions. For more information please review the 1993 Supreme Court ruling on ritual animal sacrifice and the Santeria Religion. The author and the publisher do not encourage any of the above practices nor do we assume any liabilities for presenting those formulas in this book. The formulas are presented for curious only. Neither the author nor the publisher assume any responsibilities for the outcome of any of the rituals and spells presented in this book. We make no claims to any supernatural powers of these traditional ritual ceremonies, amulets or spells. All inquiries or comments may be directed to the publisher.

TABLE OF CONTENTS

INTRODUCTION 1

SPIRITUAL INITIATIONS 4

INITIATION OF ZARABANDA 6

RITUAL CLEANSING BATH 22

EL CRISTO NEGRO 25

LOS ESPIRITUS INTRANQUILOS 26

SANTISIMA MUERTE 27

SAN SIMON 28

EL CRISTO REY 29

MADRE DE LA LUNA 30

MADRE DE AGUA 31

LA SANTISIMA PIEDRA IMAN 32

FRANCISCO DE LOS SIETE RAYOS 33

MAMA CHOLA 34

MISAS AND SPIRITUAL COMMUNICATION 35

SACRED RITUALS AND PRAYERS	39
SPIRITUAL CLEANSINGS	43
SPELLS OF PALO MAYOMBE	51
LA CASA DE LOS MUERTOS	69
SPIRITUAL CONSULTATIONS	73
RITUAL ANIMAL SACRIFICE	79
AMULETS OF PALO MAYOMBE	82
COLLARES DE PALO MAYOMBE	90
CANDLES AND FIRE	93
THE SECRETS OF THE PALO	98
SPELLS OF PALOS	108
DIRTS OF PALO MAYOMBE	123
POWDERS OF PALO MAYOMBE	125
BIBLIOGRAPHY	144

PURPOSE

The purpose of this book is to present to those of interest information about Spiritual Palo Mayombe as practiced by the Montenegro Family of both Puerto Rico and Brazil.

INTRODUCTION

Within the complex Santeria Religion, there exists a dark side called Palo Mayombe. The individual's who practice this dark aspect are called Paleros. Palo Mayombe has a long and historical history. Originating in the African Congo, the magic of Palo Mayombe was transplanted to the Caribbean during the Spanish slave trade to Puerto Rico and Cuba in the 1500's.

The Caribbean was not the only region to experience the Palo Mayombe awakening. The influence of Palo Mayombe can also be found in Brazil, Central America and in the Vera Cruz region of Mexico. Palo Mayombe in Brazil is referred to as Quimbanda. Quimbanda is a mixture of traditional Congo, Indigenous Indian and Latin American spiritualism.

There is a sharp distinction between Palo Mayombe and Santeria. The religion of Santeria uses the forces of light. The initiated members of Palo Mayombe use the forces of darkness to achieve their goals and magical spells. Because Paleros practice extremely strong and powerful black magic, many practioners of Santeria avoid being associated with Palo Mayombe.

Palo Mayombe has its own priesthood and set of rules and regulations. Rules and regulations will vary according to the guidelines of the Palo Mayombe house to which an individual has been initiated into. Although Palo Mayombe was integrated as part of the Santeria religion, it is an entirely different world rarely experienced outside of the Latin American Spiritual Community.

In these days and times, it is rare to find a sincere individual who works strictly in Palo Mayombe. The most powerful Paleros are usually found in remote villages and towns scattered throughout Latin America. In the United States there are several famous and renown Palero Priests as well as secret societies dedicated to the teachings of Palo Mayombe.

Paleros generally do not advertise their powers and will only perform spiritual work for an individual by referral. The power of many Palero Priests is so strong that they can take a man of obscure origins and turn him into a very powerful world figure in a relatively short period of time. Many of the most notorious and famous Latin American and Caribbean political leaders have been linked to an involvement with the practice of Palo Mayombe in order to keep them in power and control over the people. It is believed that a Palero can also bring death within a 24 hour period to an individual. A Palero can make or break you by saying just a few incantations and performing a few minor rituals.

There has been much publicity about Santeria in recent years, but books about Palo Mayombe are obscure and rare. The majority of the information released to the public has been negative. Information comes from individual's who are not initiated and are ignorant to factual and cultural information. Historically, ignorance or the lack of understanding has always brought fear to people. In many cases this ignorance has brought extinction to entire races of people and cultures.

It is my hope that I will be able to present to those of interest some general information and techniques about spiritual Palo Mayombe. The techniques, spells and rituals are based on the teachings of the Montenegro Family of Brazil who have been practicing this powerful magic for over 200 years.

Palo Mayombe is a very fascinating and exciting aspect of Santeria and it should not be taken lightly or ignored. I am thankful to have had the opportunity to have become a part of this ancient and beautiful form of magic. It is with great honor and pride that I salute my family and ahijados in Palo Mayombe.

SPIRITUAL INITIATIONS

When an individual decides to take the step of initiation into Spiritual Palo Mayombe, it is a life long commitment to the service and dedication to our Ancestors and Spiritual Guides. More importantly, a Palero Priest's function and role is to serve and protect the community. An individual initiated into Palo Mayombe is baptized into the secrets and mysteries of the spirit realm. Paleros say that they are born of fire and in the end will die of fire. By becoming a Palero Priest, they become a light in darkness that attracts the blessings of the spirits. In death, a Palero Priest will be extinguished by the greatest light of all, Olodumare who is God the Father. When a Palero's life is extinguished in death, they become an elevated spiritual guide of the eternal living darkness.

Before an individual can become a part of Palo Mayombe, they must first consult an experienced Palero Priest. The Palero will determine through direct contact with the spirit world and the person's ancestors if they will be able to practice Palo Mayombe. Many times the spirits will reject an individual because Palo Mayombe may not be a part of that individual's spiritual path or destiny. The spirits may also deny access to an individual because they may not yet be ready to handle or understand the responsibilities of being a Palero.

If the spirits respond favorably to your requests, the next step is to receive a spiritual cauldron or spiritual pot. After the invocation ceremony, the spiritual cauldron contains the secrets and powers of powerful spirits. In the Caribbean, this cauldron is called a Prenda or Nanga.

Because of the influence of Latin American spiritualism and culture on modern day Palo Mayombe, it is not uncommon to find Paleros whose Spirits or Muertos (The living dead) are kept inside of a large simple clay pot instead of the traditional large iron cauldron. The form in which you will receive your spirit will depend on the Palo Mayombe Priest or family who will be assisting or teaching you the secrets of Palo Mayombe.

Receiving the initiation and the spirits of Palo Mayombe is only the first step in a long and beautiful journey into the realm of the spirits.

INITIATION INTO THE MYSTERIES OF
ZARABANDA
(QUIMBANDA)

The spirit Zarabanda is the divine messenger of the underworld. It is through the spirit Zarabanda that mankind can communicate directly with the spirit world. The cauldron contains all of the elements necessary for the spirit Zarabanda to manifest and operate on earth. The spiritual cauldron is a microscopic world and the doorway to another dimension.

It is believed that an individual can not self initiate themselves into the secrets and mysteries of Palo Mayombe. In the ancient customs of the African Congo, when an individual was initiated, he went into the bush by himself or with an elder and collected all of the elements necessary to create this powerful spiritual world. It was done out of respect and veneration for the individual's ancestors as well as for spiritual protection. The individual's who received this initiation believed that they would be empowered with special magical powers from the spiritual world. The custom of self initiation changed when the Africans were brought to the New World. In order to regulate and create a hiarchy within the slave population, group initiations into Palo Mayombe were created.

ITEMS NECESSARY

1. ONE LARGE IRON CAULDRON
2. HOLY WATER FROM A CATHOLIC CHURCH
3. 8 LARGE PURE TOBACCO CIGARS
4. 1 LARGE BOTTLE OF RUM
5. PALO AMARGO
6. PALO VENCE BATALLA
7. PALO JINA
8. PALO NAMO
9. PALO DULCE
10. PALO HUESO
11. PALO JABON
12. PALO GUARAMO
13. PALO GUASIMO
14. PALO MUERTO
15. PALO ACEITUNO
16. PALO RAMON
17. PALO UNA DE GAT0
18. PALO GUAYABA
19. PALO PINO
20. PALO AMANSA GUAPO
21. PALO JOBOVAN
22. PALO CANPECHE
23. PALO OJANCHO
24. PALO GUAMA
25. PALO COCUYO
26. PALO ESPUELDE GALLO
27. PALO SANTO
28. PALO CAMITO

29. PALO DE CEIBA
30. PALO CAMBIA RUMBA
31. PALO JUSTICIA
32. PALO VEN A MI
33. PALO DIABLO
34. PALO ABRE CAMINO
35. SEVEN AFRICAN POWERS CANDLE 7 DAY
36. 28 SMALL BLACK CANDLES
37. ONE HUMAN SKULL
38. ONE LARGE ROUND SMOOTH STONE
39. 1 LARGE BLACK OBSIDIAN ARROWHEAD
40. DIRT FROM SEVEN CEMETERIES
41. DIRT FROM THE CROSSROADS
42. DIRT FROM THE MOUNTAINS
43. DIRT FROM THE FOREST
44. DIRT FROM A HOSPITAL
45. DIRT FROM A PRISON
46. DIRT FROM A COURTHOUSE
47. DIRT FROM YOUR BACKYARD
48. DIRT FROM A POLICE STATION
49. SEVEN RAILROAD SPIKES
50. 4 LARGE MACHETES
51. FIVE PREPARED COWRIE SHELLS
52. CASCARILLA
53. ONE LARGE BOTTLE OF WHITE RUM
54. 7 LARGE BLACK ROOSTERS
55. HUMAN BONES FROM THE RIGHT HAND
56. HUMAN BONES FROM THE LEFT HAND
57. HUMAN BONES FROM THE RIGHT FOOT
58. HUMAN BONES FROM THE LEFT FOOT
59. HUMAN BONES FROM THE LEFT LEG

60. HUMAN BONES FROM THE RIGHT LEG
61. HUMAN BONES FROM THE RIGHT ARM
62. HUMAN BONES FROM THE LEFT ARM
63. 9 DEAD SCORPIONS
64. 9 DEAD TRANATULAS
65. BONES FROM A BLACK CAT
66. BONES FROM A BLACK DOG
67. 5 LBS. MERCURY
68. 9 DEAD CENTIPEDES
69. 9 DEAD MILLIPEDES
70. 1 DEAD HORSESHOE CRAB
71. 9 DEAD BLACK WIDOW SPIDERS
72. 9 DEAD TICKS
73. 9 DEAD CAMELEON LIZARDS
74. 9 DEAD SPANISH FLIES
75. 9 DEAD MITES
76. 9 DEAD MOSQUITOS
77. 9 DEAD FLEAS
78. 9 DEAD RED ANTS
79. 9 DEAD HONEY BEES
80. 9 DEAD WASPS
81. 9 DEAD GRASS FROGS
82. 1 DEAD RATTLESNAKE WITH RATTLE
83. 1 DEAD WATER MOCCASIN
84. 9 DEAD BATS
85. 9 DEAD TERMITES
86. 1 DEAD RAVEN
87. 1 HEAD FROM A GUINEA HEN
88. 9 DEAD HUMMINGBIRDS
89. 1 DEAD LARGE BLACK RAT
90. 1 DEAD LARGE WHITE RAT
91. 1 DEAD BLACK MOUSE
92. 1 DEAD WHITE MOUSE

93. 4 LARGE IRON CROSSBOWS OF OCHOSI
94. 7 LARGE METAL IMPLEMENTS OF OGGUN
95. 9 MOUSE TRAPS
96. 9 RAT TRAPS
97. 1 LARGE BLESSED CRUCIFIX
98. 1 LARGE METAL CHAIN
99. 1 LARGE PAD LOCK WITH KEY
100. 9 SKELETON KEYS

These are the items that are needed to prepare the Spiritual Cauldron of the spirit Zarabanda. The average cost of the items needed to construct a legitimate and authentic cauldron of Zarabanda can range from $3500 to $4500. These items may vary according to the tradition of the Casa De Los Espiritus (Palo Mayombe Temple).

If another Palero is constructing your spiritual cauldron, you must be extremely cautious and make sure that he is legitimate and has a good reputation within the Palo Mayombe community. I have seen many individual's initiated into Palo Mayombe whose spiritual cauldrons contained nothing but unconsecrated rocks, sticks and commercial potting plant soils. If a spiritual cauldron is prepared in the incorrect manner, it will be detrimental to the individual's success, happiness , health and spiritual success. The cost to dismantle a spiritual cauldron that has been prepared incorrectly sometimes is more than the cost to put one together.

This formula and the following initiation method has been used with great success and has produced extremely powerful magical results for the individual's initiated into the Montenegro Casa De Los Espiritus.

PREPARATION

FRIDAY 11:00 P.M.
DAY 1

1. Place the iron cauldron in a location where it will not be disturbed during the 7 day initiation period. Most Paleros recommend buying a large outside metal shed that sits right on top of the open ground. If you have a basement, this would be the perfect location. If you live in an apartment, a room that you do not sleep in or is not frequently occupied.

2. Paint the symbol of Zarabanda with white paint on the inside bottom of the iron cauldron.

3. After the paint has dried, wash with holy water from a Roman Catholic Church .

4. Take a mouthful of rum and spray it directly into the iron cauldron. Do this 3 times.

5. After spraying the inside of the cauldron with the rum, light a cigar and blow the smoke directly into the cauldron. Do this three times. After you have done these first steps, the cauldron has been purified, baptized and is ready to receive the spirit.

6. Place all of the different dirts into the cauldron.

7. Add all of the mercury into the cauldron.

8. Place the large smooth stone on top of the different dirts.

9. Place items 63, 64, 65, 66, 67, 68, 69, 70, 71, 72, 73, 74, 75, 76, 77, 78, 79, 80, 81, 82, 83, 84, 85, 86, 87, 88, 89, 90, 91, and 92 into the cauldron surrounding the large smooth stone.

10. Place the large arrowhead into the cauldron.

11. Place the human skull on top of the stone.

12. Place all of the other human bones around the skull.

13. Place the seven railroad spikes into the cauldron. The pointed end of the spikes should be facing down into the dirt.

14. Place all of the palos into the cauldron. The palos should be sticking out.

15. After you have finish placing all of the Palos into the cauldron, place the machetes into the cauldron. The machetes should be placed in the directions of North, South, East and West.

16. Place the large metal implements of the Orisha Oggun into the cauldron.

17. Place the large iron crossbows from the Orisha Ochosi into the cauldron.

18. Place items 95 and 96 into the cauldron.

19. Place item 100 into the cauldron.

20. Place the large blessed crucifix into the cauldron. The crucifix should be placed towards the rear of the cauldron so that it purtruds over the back of the skull.

21. Place the five prepared Cowrie shells in a dish in front of the cauldron. These Cowrie shells will be used as a divination tool in a later chapter.

22. Go over your check list to make sure that you have everything in the cauldron before proceeding to the next step.

23. Wrap the large metal chain around the outside of the cauldron and lock up with a large pad lock. The keys to the padlock should be kept in a secret location.

12:00 MIDNIGHT

24. Using the cascarilla, make a large circle around the cauldron.

25. Place four black candles around the cauldron.

26. Light the candles in honor of the spirit that will posses the cauldron.

27. Stand in front of the cauldron

28. Light the cigar and blow the smoke directly into the cauldron. Do this 3 times.

29. Open the bottle of rum. Take a mouthful of the rum and spray it directly into the cauldron. Do this 3 times.

30. Salute the spirits by criss crossing your hands and saying the following prayer.

Sala Malecun
Malecun Sala

Zarabanda Brillumbi Indoki Inferno Viva Mundo
Zarabanda Brillumbi Indoki Inferno Viva Mundo
Zarabanda Brillumbi Indoki Inferno Viva Mundo

Who is the greatest in Heaven? Olodumare

Who are you ? Zarabanda
Who are you ? Zarabanda
Who are you ? Zarabanda

O mighty spirit Zarabanda,

I call your spirit from the North.
(Tap on the ground 3 times in front of the cauldron).

I call your spirit from the South.
(Tap on the ground 3 times in front of the cauldron).

I call your spirit from the East.
(Tap on the ground 3 times in front of the cauldron).

I call your spirit from the West.
(Tap on the ground 3 times in front of your cauldron).

O mighty Zarabanda, send your spirit to unlock the doors and mysteries from above and below.

I call upon the spirit of my Ancestors to be present and take possession of this spiritual cauldron. I do this with great honor and respect to the dead. I call you into this world to be my spiritual guide and protector. By empowering me with your supernatural strength and divine power, I will glorify your name forever.

31. Take the black rooster and sever its head.

32. Allow the blood to drip over the contents of the cauldron and also over the dish containing the cowrie shells.

33. Pull some of the roosters tail feathers out and place them inside the cauldron.

34. Light the Seven African Powers candle and place it next to the cauldron.

35. When the black candles have finished burning, place a dark piece of cloth material over the cauldron. The Spirit of Zarabanda is feeding.

SATURDAY 12:00 MIDNIGHT
INITIATION
DAY 2

1. Uncover the spiritual cauldron.

2. Stand in front of the spiritual cauldron.

3. Repeat steps 28 through 33 from day 1.

4. After saying the prayer, meditate on the powers and spiritual energies radiating from the spiritual cauldron.

5. Cover the spiritual cauldron with the cloth.

SUNDAY 12:00 MIDNIGHT
INITIATION
DAY 3

1. Uncover the spiritual cauldron.

2. Salute the spirit of Zarabanda with the same prayer used on day 1 of the initiation period.

3. Repeat steps 28 through 33 from day 1.

4. Meditate on the mysteries of Palo Mayombe.

5. Cover the spiritual cauldron with the dark cloth.

MONDAY 12:00 MIDNIGHT
INITIATION
DAY 4

1. Uncover the spiritual cauldron.

2. Stand in front of the spiritual cauldron.

3. Salute the spirit of Zarabanda with the same prayer recited on day 1 of initiation.

4. Repeat steps 28 through 33 from day 1.

TUESDAY 12:00 MIDNIGHT
INITIATION
DAY 5

1. Uncover the spiritual cauldron.

2. Salute the spirit of Zarabanda with the same prayer recited on day 1 of the initiation period.

3. Repeat steps 28 through 33 from day 1.

4. Cover the spiritual cauldron with the dark cloth.

WEDNESDAY 12:00 MIDNIGHT
INITIATION
DAY 6

1. Uncover the spiritual cauldron.

2. Salute the spirit of Zarabanda with the same prayer recited on day 1 of the initiation period.

3. Repeat steps 28 through 33 from day 1.

4. Cover the spiritual cauldron with the dark cloth.

THURSDAY 12:00 MIDNIGHT INITIATION DAY 7

1. Uncover the spiritual cauldron.

2. Salute the spirit of Zarabanda using the same prayer from day 1.

3. Repeat steps 27 through 33 from day 1.

4. Meditate on the mysteries of Palo Mayombe.

5. Cover the spiritual cauldron with the dark cloth. This is the last night of the initiation ceremony. After covering the spiritual cauldron of Zarabanda, it is recommend to take a ritual cleansing bath.

Ritual Cleansing Bath

INGREDIENTS

1. Goat's Milk
2. Lime Juice
3. Ruda
4. Santeria Kosher Rock Salt
5. Pomergranant Juice
6. Holy Water
7. White Candle

PREPARATION

1. Boil the Ruda in one gallon of water.

2. Allow the mixture to cool.

3. Strain the liquid from the mixture into a large bowl.

4. Add the lime juice to the liquid mixture.

5. Add the Pomergranant juice to the liquid mixture.

6. Add the Santeria Kosher Rock Salt to the liquid mixture.

7. Add the Holy Water to the liquid mixture.

8. Add the goat's milk to the liquid mixture.

9. Light the white candle.

10. Pour the liquid mixture into your bath water.

Remain in the bath water for 30 minutes. Most Paleros recommend to not work in any form of magic for at least three days after this cleansing bath to give your body a chance to regain its energy.

Congratulations,

Once you have completed this first and important initiation step, you will be able to start your long journey into the magic and mysteries of Palo Mayombe.

INITIATION CEREMONY OF EL CRISTO NEGRO

The initiation Ceremony of El Cristo Negro is common in Central America as well as in Mexico. El Cristo Negro is the Lord and King of the underworld. All spirits of Palo Mayombe must bow down before him. He is represented in the form of a crucified black Christ. The mysteries of El Cristo Negro are received in a very intense three day ceremony. This is one of the most powerful initiations that can be received by an individual who has been initiated into Palo Mayombe or black magic. The secrets and power of El Cristo are received inside of a large black ceramic pot. He is symbolized by black roosters and also crows. The collares of El Cristo Negro consist of three black beads, one silver bead and three clear beads. This initiation ceremony can only be performed once a year starting three days before the Roman Catholic Rite of Easter.

INITIATION CEREMONY OF THE LOS ESPIRITUS INTRANQUILOS

Los Espiritus Intranquilos or the Seven Intranquil Spirits are used in many rituals and spells common in Mexican and Central American witchcraft. The ceremony in which an individual is initiated into the mysteries of the Seven Intranquil Spirits takes place over a period of seven nights. The mysteries and secrets are received in a large black, blue and purple colored ceramic pot. When an individual receives the mysteries of the Seven Intranquil Spirits, they will be empowered to work with very strong cemetery spirits who can assist in black magic spells. The collares of the Seven Intranquil Spirits consist of seven multicolored beads and one large black onyx bead. This initiation ceremony usually takes place during the start of a new or full moon.

INITIATION CEREMONY OF SANTISIMA MUERTE

One of the most beautiful initiation ceremonies is that of the Santisima Muerte. This lengthy ceremony last for seven days and nights. This ceremony is equalvalant to the initiation ceremony in the Santeria religion called making the saint. This ritual initiation ceremony comes from the Vera Cruz region of Mexico. The Santisima Muerte is the Goddess of the Cemetery and of Death. Her powers and historical origins can be traced back to pre-Aztec era. Santisima Muerte is the chief spiritual force used by Mexican spiritualists and witches for a variety of different types of magical works. The initiates of the Santisima Muerte are usually single as the Santisima Muerte is an extremely jealous spirit. The mysteries of the Santisima Muerte are received inside of a large gold, black and red ceramic pot. The Santisima Muerte and El Cristo Negro work well together and usually the spirits will require an individual to receive both of them. The collares of the Santisima Muerte consists of seven red beads, seven clear beads and seven black beads.

INITIATION CEREMONY OF
SAN SIMON

San Simon is a very powerful spiritual force in the world of Palo Mayombe and Central American Black Magic. San Simon is the keeper to the Laws of Divine Justice. The ritual and initiation of the mysteries of San Simon originated in the Blue Fields region of Nicaragua. San Simon's initiation ceremony takes place for three nights and it includes a very large fiesta in honor of this extremely powerful spirit. When an individual becomes a priest or priestess to the powers of San Simon, they receive the power, knowledge and secrets to Divine Justice. The mysteries of San Simon are received inside of a medium size black and white ceramic pot. The collares of San Simon consists of three black beads and three white beads. Many priests initiated into the mysteries of San Simon also have a medium size iron cauldron that is said to contain the heart to the dark side of this powerful spirit. San Simon is the most powerful spirit that a Central American black magician can be initiated into. This ceremony also gives an individual the power of invisibility from the law. This initiation ceremony is rarely performed outside of the Central American region and there are very few individual's in the United States or Europe who have received it.

INITIATION CEREMONY
OF
EL CRISTO REY

El Cristo Rey is the Lord Of The World. He is the direct contact between man and God. He is associated with spells of Divine Justice, harvest, fertility and healing. A Palero will receive the initiation of El Cristo Rey to reverse witchcraft and also for spiritual alignment. The initiation ceremony of El Cristo Rey takes place for a period of three days. This ceremony gives an individual great healing powers, telepathy and the power to work with white light spirits. The mysteries of El Cristo Rey are received inside of a large white, gold and red colored ceramic pot. The collares of El Cristo Rey consists of seven white beads, one gold bead and seven red beads. This initiation ceremony has also been known to heal terminally ill individual's.

INITIATION CEREMONY OF
MADRE DE LA LUNA

The Madre De La Luna is the Goddess Of The Moon and of Los Brujos De Las Noches (Witches Of The Night). She is most often identified in Mexican Witchcraft as Nuestra Senora De La Luna. The initiation ceremony of the Madre De La Luna takes place in a field at night. This initiation ceremony never takes place unless there is a full moon. This initiation ceremony is performed in many remote parts of Mexico by Mexican witches. During the initiation, the initiate will receive the sacred knife which contains the power to the mysteries of the Madre De La Luna. This sacred knife is a powerful amulet for performing love spells. Without this knife an individual consecrated into the mysteries of Madre De La Luna is powerless. The collares of Madre De La Luna consist of pure quartz crystal beads with one crystal skull. She is sometimes identified as an owl by her initiates.

INITIATION CEREMONY OF MADRE DE AGUA

The spirit Madre De Agua is one of the most powerful spirits in Traditional Palo Mayombe. The mysteries of Madre De Agua are received in an initiation ceremony inside of a traditional Santeria Sopera. The powerful Madre De Agua is known in Palo Mayombe to posses the secrets to strong love and money magic. Many Paleros say that with Madre De Agua, you you can have anyone you desire as a lover. The Madre De Agua is also used in other powerful magical works. The collares of Madre De Agua consists of seven multi-colored beads, two clear beads, one coral colored bead and three blue beads.

INITIATION CEREMONY OF
LA SANTISIMA PIEDRA IMAN

La Santisima Piedra Iman is a very powerful spirit in Traditional Palo Mayombe. The powers of this spirit are used in both black and white magic. The spirit is used to attract money and wealth. This spirit is used by many businessmen in Latin America to achieve tremendous wealth and prosperity. The mysteries of this spirit are received inside a large ceramic pot. The collares of this spirit consists of three green beads, three clear beads and three black beads.

INITIATION CEREMONY OF FRANCISCO DE LOS SIETE RAYOS

The initiation ceremony of the spirit Francisco De Los Siete Rayos (Francisco of the Seven Rays) is one of the most ancient and traditional ceremonies in Caribbean Palo Mayombe. The mysteries and secrets of this powerful spirit who rules the four winds are received in either an iron cauldron or a large deep Terra Cotta bowl. The cost of this initiation ranges from $2500 to $3500.

INITIATION CEREMONY OF
MAMA CHOLA

This powerful female spirit is used in spells of love and fertility. This is one of the traditional spirits received in the practice of Palo Mayombe from the Caribbean. This ceremony is not common in Central American nor Brazilian Quimbanda. The cost of this initiation ceremony ranges from $1500 to $2500.

MISAS AND SPIRITUAL COMMUNICATION

The Spiritual Misa of Palo Mayombe is the most important part of the Palo Mayombe religion. It is through a misa that you will be able to communicate directly with the spirits of Palo Mayombe. It is also through your first Palo Mayombe Misa that the names of many of your ancestor's spirits will be revealed. There are other types of misas in Santeria, but the Misa of Palo Mayombe should only be done alone or with other initiates of Palo Mayombe. By having these frequent meetings with your spirits, the bound between the two of you will grow stronger. During a misa, many strange supernatural events and visions may take place. Do not be alarmed of these events, it is only the spirits revealing their power to you.

HOW TO CONDUCT A PALO MAYOMBE MISA

1. Draw a large circle of cascarilla around an area on the ground.

2. The circle must be large enough so you can place a chair inside the circle.

3. Place 13 red candles around the circle.

4. Light the candles.

5. Place the spiritual cauldron into the circle.

6. Place a chair inside of the circle facing the spiritual cauldron.

7. Tap the ground in front of the spiritual cauldron three times.

8. Uncover the cauldron.

9. Light a cigar and blow the smoke directly into the cauldron.

10. Take a mouthful of white rum and spray it directly into the cauldron.

11. Salute the spirit by criss crossing your hands and saying the initiation prayer.

12. After the opening prayer, sit down and say the following prayers.

We believe in one God,
The Father, the Almighty
maker of Heaven and Earth,
of all that is seen and unseen.
We believe in El Cristo Rey,
the only son of Olodumare,
eternally begotten of the Father
God from God, Light from Light,
true God from true God,
begotten, not made, one in being with the
Father. Through him all things were

made. For us men and for our salvation
he came down from heaven,
by the power of the Holy Spirit he
was born of the Most Holy Mother the Virgin Mary,
and he became man. For our sake
he was crucified.

He suffered, died, and was buried. He
descended into hell and conquered the
angel of death and took his rightful
place as the Lord Of The Underworld. On
the third day he rose again in fulfillment
of the prophecies, he ascended into Heaven
and is seated at the right hand of Olodumare.
El Cristo Rey will come again in glory to
judge the living and the dead, and his kingdom
will have no end. We believe in the Holy
Spirit, the Lord, the giver of life, who
proceeds from the Father and the Son.
With the Father and the Son he worshiped
and glorified. He has spoken through the
Prophets. We look for the resurrection
of the dead, and the life of the world to come.
AMEN
Our Father who art in Heaven,
hallowed by thy name, thy kingdom
come, thy will be done on earth as it
as it is in Heaven. Give us this day our daily
bread, and forgive us our trespasses
as we forgive those who trespass
against us, and lead us not into
temptation, but deliver us from evil.
AMEN

O powerful Spirit, I ask you to reveal
yourself to me. I ask you in the name
of all those who have come before you.
O powerful Spirit, you are born of fire
and dwell in my eternal soul. Reveal
your power and sacred mysteries to
me in the name of El Cristo Negro and
El Cristo Rey.

AMEN

13. Meditate and close your eyes.

14. The spirits will speak to you through visions and sometimes you will even be able to see and hear the spirits.

This Spiritual Palo Mayombe Misa should be done on a weekly basis. It may take some time before the spirits have enough confidence in you to reveal their secrets to you. When they begin sharing their mysteries with you, your life will be changed forever.

CLOSING THE SPIRITUAL PALO MAYOMBE MISA

O powerful and eternal Spirit, I thank you for
revealing the secrets of your mighty wisdom with
me. I respect you and honor your great power. I
ask for your protection and divine power to be with
me for all eternity.

SACRED RITUALS AND PRAYERS

The rituals and prayers of Palo Mayombe are simple but yet complex. Performing rituals with the spirits is a serious and important aspect of Palo Mayombe. The more time that you spend working with the spirits, the more benefits you will receive. The spirits will never give you a situation that you can not handle, although be ready to prove your allegiance to them. If you fail them, it may be a long time before you regain their confidence. The further you go into Palo Mayombe, the more rituals you will need to learn. If you have a good Madrina or Padrino in Palo Mayombe they will be able to teach you and tell you when you are ready to receive the next initiation of Palo Mayombe. For the beginner of Palo Mayombe, I have included just a few prayers and rituals to get you started.

SALUTING THE SPIRIT OF ZARABANDA

This is how you should salute your spiritual cauldron each and every time you come before it. You should do this at least twice a week. If you will be working strictly with the forces of Palo Mayombe, you will need to do this on a daily basis. The best time to do this is in the morning hours before seeing your first client.

PROCEDURE

1. Tap on the ground in front of the spiritual cauldron three times. This signals the spirit that it is you.

2. Uncover the cloth from the spiritual cauldron.

3. Light a cigar and blow the smoke directly into the cauldron.

4. Take a mouthful of rum and spray it directly into the cauldron.

5. Stand in front of the spiritual cauldron.

6. Salute the spirits by criss crossing your hands and saying the following prayer.

Sala Malecun
Malecun Sala

Zarabanda Brillumbi Indoki Inferno Viva Mundo
Zarabanda Brillumbi Indoki Inferno Viva Mundo
Zarabanda Brillumbi Indoki Inferno Viva Mundo

Who is the greatest in heaven? Olodumare

Who are you? Zarabanda
Who are you? Zarabanda
Who are you? Zarabanda

O mighty spirit Zarabanda, I ask you to protect me and guide me in my life. I honor you and give your divine name honor. Circle my body and home with a ring of powerful fire to protect me from my enemies and to balance nature in my favor.

RITUAL FOR DIVINE JUSTICE

1. Salute the spirit of the cauldron.

2. Recite the ritual prayer of Zarabanda.

3. Place a ring of red candles (7) around the spiritual cauldron.

4. Light the candles.

5. Recite the following prayer.

O saving spirit of the mighty Zarabanda, open wide the gates of heaven to us below, our enemies press on from every side. Do not allow the capture of my soul. By offending me they are offending you. Balance the scales of justice in our favor. To your great name and power be endless praise, Immortal Spirit, one in thee, grant me salvation and triumph in the battle of our enemies.

RITUAL FOR REVERSING WITCHCRAFT

1. Salute the spirit of the cauldron.

2. Recite the ritual prayer of Zarabanda.

3. Light a 14 day reverse candle and place it next to the cauldron.

4. Recite the following prayer.

O powerful spirit Zarabanda, born of fire and of man, I seek your deliverance and protection from the Mothers of the Night. I ask you to enter into my body and to make right what is not. You are all powerful and all knowing. Reverse what has been done and send it back to the source, destroying the creator of this sin. Defender of the Realm of El Cristo Negro and of Earth do not let this evil consume us. To your great name be endless praise.

SPIRITUAL CLEANSINGS OF PALO MAYOMBE

When a Palero conducts a cleansing ceremony for an individual, it is usually associated with removing witchcraft or strong sorcery. Because the magic of Palo Mayombe is so strong, usually only a Palero Priest has the knowledge to remove what another Palero has done to an individual. It must be remembered that a Palero Priest works with the spirits of darkness and therefore he will use a great amount of his knowledge in the black arts as well as his own energy to save the individual. If a Palero fails, at this task at cleansing an individual, it might be his last. Spiritual cleansings are performed with a wide variety of items such as candles, spiritual waters, herbs and live animals. An experienced Palero Priest will be able to quickly determine the type of spiritual illness that plaques an individual and the necessary remedy.

TO REMOVE WITCHCRAFT OR SORCERY

This is an extremely strong spiritual cleansing. It should only be performed by a Palero who is totally competent in commanding the spirits.

INGREDIENTS

1. FOURTEEN WHITE CANDLES
2. CASCARILLA
3. RUM
4. CIGARS
5. WHITE ONIONS
6. PALO CLAVO
7. PALO CABALLERO
8. COCONUT
9. HOLY WATER
10. BLACK ROOSTER

PREPARATION

1. Grate the meat of the coconut and place it into a large bowl.

2. Pulverize the Palo Clavo and the Palo Caballero into a fine powder.

3. Mix the powder of the Palo Clavo and the Palo Caballero into the coconut mixture.

4. Mix the Holy Water into the coconut mixture.

5. Make a large circle using the Cascarilla around the individual.

6. Slice the white onion and place on top of the Cascarilla circle.

7. Make sure that the onion completely circles the individual.

8. Place the fourteen candles around the circle.

9. Light the cigar and blow the smoke into the cauldron.

10. Spray the spiritual cauldron with the rum.

11. Blindfold the individual in the middle of the circle.

12. The individual must be naked.

13. Light the fourteen candles.

14. Blow the smoke from the cigar into the circle and around the individual.

15. Spray rum onto the body of the individual.

16. Take the black rooster and cleanse the individual's body with it.

17. After cleansing the individual's body with the black rooster, sever the head of the black rooster and pour the blood directly into the cauldron of the spirit.

18. Take the coconut paste and apply it to the forehead of the individual. Tie a white or red cloth around the head of the individual. Make sure that the paste does not fall out.

20. The individual must place their old cloths into a large paper bag along with the body of the rooster.

21. Dispose of the bag with the clothes and the rooster.

22. Allow the individual to change into brand new white clothes.

23. The individual must sleep with the mixture on the head for one night.

24. The next morning the individual must take a spiritual bath consisting of milk, cascarilla and the Holy Water.

TO ESCAPE THE LAW

This cleansing is used by Paleros to remove an individual from the path of the law.

INGREDIENTS

1. TWELVE BLACK CANDLES
2. HOLY WATER
3. AGUARDIENTE
4. CIGAR
5. POLVO DE LOS MUERTOS
6. MILK
7. TWO BLACK ROOSTERS
8. LARGE METAL BASIN
9. CASCARILLA
10. ONE SET OF PREPARED COLLARES DE EGUN

PREPARATION

1. Mix the Holy Water, milk and the Aguardiente together in a large bowl.

2. Make a large circle using the Cascarilla.

3. Place the black candles around the outer circle.

4. Place the large metal basin in the center of the circle.

5. The individual must stand naked in the metal basin.

6. Blindfold the individual.

7. Light the candles.

8. Cleanse the individual with the rooster.

9. Present the black rooster to the spirit of the cauldron and sever its head.

10. Allow the blood to drip into the cauldron.

11. Take the other black rooster and cleanse the body of the individual.

12. After the cleansing, sever the head of the rooster and pour the blood into the Holy Water mixture.

13. Pour the Holy Water and blood mixture over the top of the individual.

14. The individual should change into new white clothes and be presented with the Collares of Egun.

SPIRITUAL CLEANSING AGAINST DEATH

This spiritual cleansing is used to prolong a person's life.

INGREDIENTS

1. TWENTY ONE WHITE CANDLES
2. MEDIUM COLORED ROOSTER
3. TWENTY ONE MULTI COLORED RIBBONS
4. TWENTY ONE PENNIES
5. RED CLOTH
6. CIGAR RUM

PREPARATION

1. Make a circle with the candles around the individual.

2. Blindfold the individual.

3. Light the candles.

4. Cleanse the individual with the rooster.

5. After cleansing the individual, cut the head off the rooster and pour the blood into the cauldron of the spirit.

6. Tie the rooster, the pennies and the ribbons in the red cloth.

7. Spray the red cloth with rum.

8. Place the red cloth containing the Rooster into a brown paper bag.

9. Blow some cigar smoke into the bag before closing it.

10. Take the package to the cemetery and bury it before 12:00 Midnight.

This cleansing should be done during a Spiritual Misa or around 9:00 P.M.

SPELLS OF
PALO MAYOMBE

The success of spells depends upon the experience that the Palero has acquired. If you are just beginning or have been initiated, do not expect miracles over night. In time as you work closely with the spirits, you will even amaze yourself. The following spells are taken from my own Libretta. They are not to be taken lightly. Please review each spell with a clear mind and do not rush into anything.

THE BOMB

This spell is used to destroy the foundation of an individual. This spell is so powerful that even the most experienced Santero or Palero would have difficulty removing it from an individual. There is no known antidote for this spell.

INGREDIENTS

1. ONE LARGE DARK BOTTLE
2. WHITE VINEGAR
3. URINE
4. PALO VENCE BATALLA
5. PALO MUERTO
6. POLVO DE LOS MUERTOS
7. POLVO DE ESCORPION
8. GUN POWDER
9. ONE LIME
10. 72 PINS
11. BLACK CANDLE

PREPARATION

1. Always begin by saluting your spirits.

2. Write the person's name on a brown piece of paper three times.

3. Cut the lime in half, but do not separate.

4. Fold the paper with the individual's name and place between the lime.

5. Take the 72 pins and insert them all around the lime making sure that it will not separate.

6 . Place the lime into the dark bottle.

7. Pour the urine into the bottle.

8. Place the Palo Vence Batalla and the Palo Muerto into the bottle.

9. Add the white vinegar to the bottle.

10. Add the Polvo De Escorpion and the Polvo De Los Muertos to the liquid mixture of the bottle.

11. Place the top back on the bottle and then shake seven times.

12. Go to the cemetery and dig a medium size hole over a grave.

13. Open the bottle and add the the Gun Powder into the liquid mixture of the bottle. Quickly bury the bottle over the grave.

14. Light the Black Candle and place it in the center of the dirt mound.

15. When you arrive back home, it is necessary to take a cleansing bath to remove any negative vibration that could have been picked up at the cemetery.

This spell usually has fast results. You should start to see the spell beginning to affect the person within seven days.

TO DOMINATE AN INDIVIDUAL

INGREDIENTS

1. ONE BLACK WAX IMAGE CANDLE
2. DOMINATION OIL
3. PALO ACEITUNO
4. PALO UNA DE GAT0
5. RED THREAD
6. SUGAR CANE LEAVES
7. CASCARILLA
8. 12 SMALL RED CANDLES

PREPARATION

1. Carve the complete name of the individual three times on the wax image candle.

2. Anoint the wax image with the domination oil.

3. Using the red thread, tie the Palo Aceituno and the Palo Una De Gato around the wax image.

4. Take the leaves of the sugar cane and completely wrap the wax image and the palos.

5. Wrap the red thread around the sugar cane leaves so the leaves are completely covered in red thread.

6. Make a medium size circle around the wax image package using the cascarilla.

7. Place the candles around the outer circle.

8. Light the candles while invoking the spirits.

9. Allow the candles to completely burn out.

10. Place the wax figure package near the cauldron of your spirit.

11. As long as you have this magic package near your spirits they will allow you to dominate the individual as well as the guardian angel of the individual. If the magic package is opened, the spell will be released.

TO SEPARATE TWO PEOPLE

This spell is used to break up lovers, friendships and marriages.

INGREDIENTS

1. PALO MUERTO
2. PALO OJANCHO
3. POLVO DE LOS MUERTOS
4. FOURTEEN LARGE NAILS
5. SAL NEGRA (BLACK SALT)
6. THREE PULVERIZED LIMES
7. MILK
8. TWO IMAGE CANDLES
9. BLACK THREAD
10. SEVEN SMALL BLACK CANDLES
11. ONE LARGE WIDE MOUTH JAR
12. TIERRA DE LOS MUERTOS

PREPARATION

1. Take the two image candles to a Catholic Church and using the Holy Water in the church, baptize the figures in the name of the individual's.

2. Carve the names of the individual's into the wax images.

3. Take the Palo Muerto and the Palo Ojancho and place it between the two wax images.

4. The two images should not be facing each other.

5. Using the black thread, tie the two figures and the Palos together tightly.

6. Place the wax figures into the jar.

7. Place seven nails into the jar.

8. Place the pulverized limes into the jar.

9. Place the the Polvo De Los Muertos into the jar.

10. Add the Black Salt to the mixture.

11. Pour the milk into the jar.

12. Place one of the black candles on the top of the jar.

13. Light the black candle.

14. A candle should be lit each day for seven days.

15. Pulverize some of the Palo Ojancho and place it in a small pouch.

16. Add the other seven nails to the pouch.

17. Add the Tierra De Los Muertos to the pouch.

18. On the seventh day of the spell, take this mixture and drop it near the person's house.

This spell should be done between the hours of 9:00 p.m. and 12:00 midnight. It will take seven to ten days before the conflicts begin between the two individual's.

TO MAKE AN INDIVIDUAL SICK

INGREDIENTS

1. PALO PINO
2. PALO MULATTO
3. PALO BOMBA
4. DIRTY STREET WATER
5. FOURTEEN EARTH WORMS
6. SEVEN BLACK CANDLES
7. MEDIUM SIZE JAR
8. AGUARDIENTE

PREPARATION

1. Take a picture of the individual and write their name on the back three times.

2. Place the picture into the jar.

3. Place the Palo Pino into the jar.

4. Place the Palo Mulatto into the jar.

5. Place the Palo Bomba into the jar.

6. Pour the dirty street water into the jar.

7. Pour the Aguardiente into the jar.

8. Place the fourteen earth worms into the liquid mixture.

9. Cover the jar with its top.

10. Invoke the spirit of the cauldron.

11. Light a black candle near the jar for seven days.

12. After the seven days take the jar to the cemetery and bury it over a grave.

The individual will usually develop stomach or severe intestinal problems. This spell can only be reversed using strong Santeria cleansing baths or ceremonies. If the sick individual does not believe in Santeria or Palo Mayombe, it is certain that the condition could lead to even more complicated health problems.

TO MAKE AN INDIVIDUAL LOSE THEIR JOB

This is a very strong spell to make an individual leave or lose their job.

INGREDIENTS

1. PALO DIABLO
2. PALO MUERTO
3. SAL NEGRA
4. BLACK CLOTH
5. BLACK CANDLE
6. BLACK THREAD
7. POLVO DE TORO

PREPARATION

1. Write the individual's name on a brown piece of paper three times.

2. Wrap the brown piece of paper tightly around the Palo Muerto and the Palo Diablo.

3. Tie the palos together with black thread.

4. Place the palos on top of the black cloth.

5. Place the Polvo De Toro and the Sal Negra on top of the Palos.

6. Wrap the Palos together with the Polvo De Toro and the Sal Negra in the black cloth.

7. Place the black cloth bundle into a large Terra Cotta dish.

8. Light the black candle.

9. Invoke the dark spirits.

10. After the candle has completely burned out, saturate the black cloth bundle with lighter fluid.

11. Set the bundle on fire.

12. After it has finished burning, pulverize the remains into a fine powder.

13. Take the powder and drop it in the work place of the individual. If you can, try and place some of the powder into the individual's pocket or work clothes.

PALO MAYOMBE HOLY WATER

This Palo Mayombe Holy Water is used by a Palero or Spiritualist to multiply the supernatural forces of the Dark Spirits. The Holy Water can be used to give a Palero extra power and strength when divining or preparing a magic spell. This water is also good for seances and the Misa De Palo Mayombe.

INGREDIENTS

1. PALO AMARGO
2. PALO RAMON
3. PALO GUAMO
4. POLO COCUYO
5. SEVEN DIFFERENT COLORED RIBBONS
6. MAY RAIN WATER
7. LARGE EMPTY WINE BOTTLE WITH TOP

PREPARATION

1. Place all of the Palos into the empty wine bottle.

2. Pour the May rain water into the bottle.

3. Tie the ribbons around the neck of the wine bottle.

4. Allow the mixture to stand for seven days before using.

TO TIE A LOVER DOWN

This spell will keep a lover tied to you even against their will.

INGREDIENTS

1. PALO DULCE
2. PALO AMANSA GUAPO
3. PALO SANTO
4. PALO CAMITO
5. RED WINE
6. HONEY
7. CINNAMON STICKS
8. LARGE CALABASA LEAF
9. MEDIUM WIDE MOUTH JAR
10. RED CANDLE

PREPARATION

1. Write your name three times on a brown piece of paper.

2. Write the other individual's name across your name three times. The names should cross each other in the form of a cross.

3. Fold the brown paper into a tiny square.

4. Place the folded paper between all of the Palos.

5. Tie the palos together with red thread.

6. Wrap the palos in the Calabasas leaf.

7. Wrap the calabasa leaf with red thread.

8. Place the calabasas leaf into the jar.

9. Pour the honey over the calabasas leaf.

10. Pour the red wine into the jar.

11. Place the cinnamon sticks into the jar around the calabasas leaf.

12. Place the top of the jar on tightly.

13. Light the red candle and invoke your spirit.

14. After the candle has completely burned out, place the jar in a dark hidden location.

TO RELEASE SOMEONE FROM JAIL

This spell is used to get someone out of jail.

INGREDIENTS

1. PALO AMARGO
2. PALO JOBOVAN
3. PALO JUSTICIA
3. EARTH FROM FOUR JAILS
4. POLVO DE VENADO
5. CASCARILLA
6. 28 SMALL RED CANDLES
7. RUM
8. SEVEN CIGARS
9. ONE BLACK ROOSTER
10. SEVEN DIFFERENT COLORED SPOOLS OF THREAD.

PREPARATION

1. Salute your spirit with the traditional prayers and offerings.

2. Draw a medium circle with the cascarilla in front of the spiritual cauldron.

3. Draw a cross in the middle of the circle that connects to the outer edges.

4. The middle of the cross will be the focus point of power for the spell.

5. Place four of the candles around the outer circle.

6. Write the individual's name on a brown piece of paper.

7. Wrap the paper around the Palo Amargo, Palo Justicia and the Palo Jobovan.

8. Tie the palos together with seven different colored threads.

9. Place the Palos in the center of the circle.

10. Mix the Polvo De Venado and the Earth Of Four Jails together in a bowl.

11. Form a mound using this mixture over the palos.

12. Invoke the spirits of darkness for assistance.

13. Light the candles.

14. Spray the rum over your magic work.

15. Light the cigar and blow the smoke into the circle.

16. Cut the head off the black rooster and pour the blood into the cauldron and over the earth mound in the middle of the circle.

17. The candles should be lit for seven days.

18. At the end of seven days, the mixture should be buried near the jail where the individual is incarcerated.

LA CASA DE LOS MUERTOS

La Casa De Los Muertos or the House Of The Dead is where the spirits of Palo Mayombe reside. Because the forces and the power of the dark spirits are so fierce, they can not be kept with a Santero's Santos or other spiritual guides. Traditionally, a Palero will keep his spirits in a special outside house or even in a metal shed. This special house must have a lock to keep away curious people. The house must be large enough to conduct your dark magic or misas. If you live in an apartment, you must keep your spirits in a seperate room or in a closet large enough for them. A basement is the perfect place for working with the spirits of Palo Mayombe. If you receive other spirits of Palo Mayombe, they can be kept together. There should be a minimum amount of light and at least one candle burning in honor of the spirits at all times. La Casa De Los Muertos should be well stocked with the traditional supplies and magical elixirs of a Palero. The following is a list of supplies that you should keep with your spirits.

1. TIERRA DE LOS MUERTOS
2. POLVO DE GANGA
3. AGUARDIENTE
4. CIGARS
5. COMPLETE STOCK OF PALOS
6. POLVO DE TORO
7. POLVO DE VENADO
8. MULTICOLORED RIBBONS
9. PALO MAYOMBE HOLY WATER
10. POLVO DE LOS MUERTOS
11. VARIETY OF CANDLES
12. POLVO DE ESCORPION
13. POLVO DE CULEBRA
14. VARIETY OF POWDERED PALOS
15. VARIETY OF EMPTY JARS
16. COCONUTS
17. VARIETY OF PALO MAYOMBE HERBS
18. CASCARILLA
19. CROW FEATHERS
20. VARIETY OF OILS
21. RED CLOTH
22. BLACK CLOTH
23. VARIETY OF DIFFERENT EARTHS
24. VINEGAR
25. MARACAS
26. STONES FROM VARIOUS SOURCES
27. VARIETY OF SEA SHELLS
28. VARIETY OF BEADS
29. VARIETY OF COLORED THREADS
30. VARIETY OF DIFFERENT SIZE BOWLS
31. VARIETY OF DIFFERENT SALTS
32. LIMES
33. PINS AND NEEDLES

34. WHITE PLATES
35. CEMENT AND WAXES
36. HUMAN BONES (POWDERED & WHOLE)
37. AGUA DE PALO (ASSORTED)
38. PARCHMENT PAPER
39. BROWN LUNCH PAPER BAGS
40. DRAGON'S BLOOD
41. OLIVE OIL
42. MERCURY
43. THICK BAMBOO STICKS
44. IRON CAULDRONS (VARIOUS SIZES)
45. CHARCOAL CARBON
46. BULL HORNS
47. TURTLE SHELLS
48. PRESERVED HUMMINGBIRDS
49. BLACK ROOSTER FEET
50. BLACK CROW FEET
51. CEMENT
52. GLUE GUN
53. COWRIE SHELLS
54. DRY GOURDS
55. DRIED BATS
56. A VARIETY OF ANIMAL BONES
57. PRESERVED REPTILES AND INSECTS
58. BLACK CAT HAIR
59. BLACK DOG HAIR
60. URINE (AGED)
61. COTTON
62. RUBBING ALCOHOL
63. GUN POWDER
64. CANDLE WICKS
65. PRECIPITADO ROJO
66. PRECIPITADO BLANCO

67. PALO MAYOMBE COLLARES
68. SMALL KNIFES
69. A VARIETY OF OCHOSI BOW AND ARROWS
70. A VARIETY OF CRYSTALS

There are many more items that a Palero can use, but these are the most common.

SPIRITUAL CONSULTATIONS

The five Cowrie shells that were consecrated in the initiation ceremony can be used for communication with the spirits. The shells should be washed off, of all the blood and other sacred ingredients. By consecrating them with your spiritual cauldron, you have also given them life and a direct line to the world of the dark spirits.

PREPARATION

1. The Cowrie shells should be opened up on one side and prepared in the Santeria tradition.

2. The shells should be thrown on a straw mat or a round tightly woven wicker shallow basket.

3. There should always be a candle lit at your spiritual table.

4. There should be always a glass of fresh water with a crucifix at the spiritual table to collect the negative vibrations.

5. Palo Mayombe Holy Water, cigars and rum should always be available at your table, as the spirits sometimes have strange requests.

PROCEDURE

1. Begin by honoring the Ancestors with water. Place three drops of water on the ground and say.

>Omi Totu Ana Tutu Omi Olofin A
>Leggua Tutu Elei

2. Take the Cowrie shells and begin shaking them in both hands in a clockwise rotation.

3. Begin and open up the reading by the following prayer while shaking the shells.

>Boguo Imaworo Iyalocha Babalocha
>Babalao Oluoricha Icu Embelese Ibae
>Balleral Baye Tonu.
>
>A todos los Oluos que estan Icu Ibae.
>Kinkamache Mi Madrina
>Kinkamache Mi Padrino
>
>Kosi Icu
>Kosi Arun
>Kosi Feitibo
>Kosi Arafin

Name of the person that you are conducting the consultation for. _____.

4. After saying the name of the individual receiving the reading, begin to shake the shells in a counter clockwise rotation. Say the following words.

> Fu Mi Obon
> Fu Mi Abarra
> Fu Mi Italero
> Fu Mi Ifa

5. Give the shells to the individual and allow them to shake them in their hands. Tell the individual to concentrate.

6. When the individual has finished, take the shells back and present them to their head and both hands.

7. With the shells in your right hand, make the sign of the cross on the table.

8. After making the sign of the cross with your hand, release the shells onto the mat.

9. Mark the number down and throw the shells again.

10. Throw the shells again for the second number.

11. This first combination of numbers will tell you if the spirits are willing to speak to the individual and if the reading comes with blessings from the spirits or with warnings.

12. If the spirits do not wish to speak to the individual, the Palero must find out why and if a simple offering such as a cigar or rum can open up the communication between the individual and the spirits.

13. The Palero should always keep a record in his Libretta or the Book Of Shadows of the numbers which fall for an individual.

14. The Shells must always be thrown twice to get a combination of two numbers.

15. The shells should be read by counting the amount of shells that are open sided. That will be your number to write down.

16. A good Palo Mayombe reading should last no more than 30 minutes and it should include the spiritual remedies for the individual.

The normal cost for a reading is $21.00 to $42.00. This money should only be used to buy materials and offerings for your spirits.

SHELL COMBINATIONS AND MEANINGS

0-0 DANGER & NO; THIS READING IS NOW CLOSED
0-1 NO
0-2 NOT LIKELY
0-3 POSSIBLE BUT WITH IMPOSSIBLE ODDS
0-4 LIKELY BUT SACRIFICE MUST BE DONE
0-5 NO AND DANGER
1-1 NO
1-2 NO
1-3 YES BUT SACRIFICE MUST BE MADE
1-4 YES BUT THROW THE SHELLS AGAIN
1-5 NO AND TRAGEDY WILL SOON FOLLOW
2-1 FOR THE MOMENT YES YOU CAN
2-2 BEWARE OF HEALTH PROBLEMS
2-3 THE SUN WILL SHINE
2-4 YES, LOOK TO THE EAST
2-5 YOUR LUCK IS SOON TO WORSEN
3-0 THE DOORS ARE OPEN BUT WILL SOON CLOSE
3-1 SUCCESS COMES FROM LESSONS LEARNED
3-2 YES BUT APPROACH WITH CAUTION
3-3 YES YES YES
3-4 THE SUN WILL SHINE
3-5 PAY ATTENTION AND OPEN YOUR EYES
4-0 YOUR EMPIRE WILL SOON COLLAPSE
4-1 HONOR YOUR ANCESTORS
4-2 YES BUT ASK AGAIN

4-3 YES IN 14 DAYS
4-4 BLESSINGS FROM HEAVEN
4-5 LAUGH NOW, CRY LATER
5-1 DEATH AND TRAGEDY
5-2 SEPARATION
5-3 LEGAL AND PAPER PROBLEMS
5-4 THE ENEMY IS IN YOUR HOUSE
5-5 DEATH, TRAGEDY AND WITCHCRAFT

COMO MATAR UN GALLO
RITUAL SACRIFICE

Animal sacrifice is an important part of the rites and rituals of Palo Mayombe and to the Santeria Religion in general. The sacrifice of animals should not be taken lightly and it must be carried out in accordance with strict religious regulations. Only initiated members of Santeria and Palo Mayombe may conduct a sacrifice in the following manner. Under no circumstances must the animal be allowed to suffer as this would violate the Santeria and Palo Mayombe code of ethics.

The following procedure can be used in both Santeria as well as Palo Mayombe.

COMO MATAR UN GALLO

1. Take the rooster from its cage and say the following prayer:

> ICU MENI ICU MENI ICU MENI ICU
> MENELAN ICU MENELAN ICU MENELAN

2. Wash the feet of the rooster and say the following prayer:

> IROCUSO IROCOSOGUE, IRO IRO
> IROCUSO IRO IROCOSOGUE

3. Before the sacrifice say the following prayer.

> LLAGUINA LLAGUINA OLOSUN
>
> BARA LLAGUINA LLAGUINA OLOSUN
> BARA LLAGUINA LLAGUESE OLOSUN
>
> LLAGUESE LLAGUESE OLOSUN BARA
> LLEGUESE OGGUN CHOROCHERE
>
> ELLEVA LERCARO - *say the name of your spirit*
> ELLESE AVIAMA ELEGGUA DECUN ELELA
>
> DECUONLLE ELLEGUA DECUN ELELA
> DECUONLLE ELLEGUA DECUN ELELA
> DECUONLLE ODUMARLE ODUMARLE

4. Pull some of the neck feathers from the rooster and place them into the cauldron

5. Say the following prayer:

> TORU MALICUNI TORU MALICUNI
> TORU MALICUNI ERAUGO BOGUE
> CONI ERAUGO CUNIELLE. ACHE MI
> ELERDA ORI ARO IKU ACHE MI
> ILE TORU MALICUNI TORU MALICUNI
> ERAUGO BOGUE CONI ERAUGO
> CUNIELLE ACHE MI ILE MAFEREFUN OCHA
> TORU MALICUNI MAFEREFUN ORICHA

6. Quickly sever the head of the rooster and allow the blood to drip into the cauldron.

7. Do not forget to offer the spirits cigar smoke and their favorite drink, rum.

8. Cover the cauldron with a cloth and allow the spirits to remain feeding for a 24 hour period.

9. Light a candle in honor of the spirits.

This is the correct procedure to feed the spirits of Palo Mayombe and to perform an animal ritual sacrifice.

AMULETS OF PALO MAYOMBE

The use of amulets in Palo Mayombe is quit popular as in the Santeria community. Amulets can be prepared with various secret herbs, powders and objects. The amulets that a Palero prepares are very strong and powerful and many times contain spirits. A Palero who can prepare powerful amulets is an invaluable asset to the Santeria and Palo Mayombe community.

AMULET AGAINST DEATH AND TRAGEDY

This amulet will protect an individual from death or tragic accidents. If this amulet is hung near the front door of a home, it will protect the entire family.

INGREDIENTS

1. LARGE PIEDRA DE RAYO
2. MULTI COLORED BEADS
3. THREE BLACK ROOSTER TAIL FEATHERS
4. FOUR RED CANDLES
5. WHITE PAINT
6. RUM
7. CIGAR
8. RED WINE

PREPARATION

1. Place the Piedra De Rayo into a small bowl.

2. Salute your spirits.

3. Take a mouthful of rum and spray the Piedra De Rayo.

4. Do this three times with the rum.

5. Light the cigar and blow smoke directly onto the Piedra De Rayo.

6. Do this three times.

7. Using the white paint, paint a circle with a cross of arrows in the center. Do this on both sides.

8. String the multi colored beads on a long cotton string.

9. Rub a thin layer of adhesive glue over the Piedra De Rayo.

10. Wrap the string of beads around the Piedra De Rayo. The Piedra De Rayo must be completely covered with the beads.

11. Place the feathers in the pointed end of the Piedra De Rayo.

12. Allow the amulet to dry.

13. After it has dried, light the red candle in honor of the spirits.

14. Ask the spirits to protect the person for whom you are making the amulet for.

15. Sprinkle a good amount of the red wine over the amulet in the bowl.

16. Allow the amulet to remain until the candle has completely burned out.

When the amulet is placed in its final location, make sure that the feathers are in a upright position. This is a very powerful amulet.

AMULET FOR VICTORY OVER ENEMIES

This amulet will give an individual great supernatural power to overcome and conquer their enemies.

INGREDIENTS

1. PALO JINA
2. PALO AMARGO
3. PALO GUARAMO
4. BLACK ROOSTER
5. MULTI COLORED BEADS
6. MINIATURE METAL SWORD
7. RUM
8. CIGAR
9. MAY RAIN WATER
10. RED CANDLE

PREPARATION

1. Place the Palo Jina, Palo Amargo, Palo Guaramo and the miniature sword into a large bowl.

2. The Palos should be about 4 to 6 inches in length.

3. Salute your spirits.

4. Take a mouthful of rum and spray it directly onto the palos and the sword.

5. Do this three times.

6. Light the cigar and blow the smoke directly onto the the palos and the sword.

7. Do this three times.

8. Sever the head of the rooster and allow the blood to drip directly onto the palos and the sword.

9. Place the four red candles around the bowl.

10. Light the red candle in honor of the spirits.

11. Pour May Rain Water over the palos and the sword.

12. Allow the mixture to stand for 24 hours.

13. String the multi colored beads onto a long cotton string.

14. After the 24 hours, remove the palos and the metal sword.

15. Bundle the palos around the metal sword.

16. Apply a thin layer of adhesive glue onto the palos and then completely wrap the bundle with the string of beads.

17. Allow the glue to dry.

This amulet should be kept in an individual's pocket or purse. This powerful amulet has never failed any of my clients or Ahijados.

AMULET TO ESCAPE THE LAW

This is a very famous and powerful amulet that allows an individual to escape the law or avoid legal problems. This amulet can also be used to win a court case.

INGREDIENTS

1. EARTH OF THE MOUNTAINS 1/4 OZ.
2. EARTH OF THE CROSSROADS 1/4 OZ.
3. EARTH OF FOUR JAILS 1/4 OZ.
4. EARTH OF FOUR POLICE STATIONS 1/4 OZ.
5. POLVO DE VENADO 1/4 OZ.
6. PALO JOBOVAN
7. PALO COCUYO
8. MEDIUM SIZE HOLLOW DEER ANTLER
9. BLACK ROOSTER
10. ONE DARK PIGEON
11. SEVEN MULTI COLORED BEADS
12. ONE COWRIE SHELL
13. FOUR RED CANDLES
14. MINIATURE SMOOTH STONE FROM THE MONTE

PREPARATION

1. Place all of the earth's into a large bowl.

2. Add the Polvo De Venado to the earth mixture.

3. Add the one inch Palo Jobovan and the Palo Cocuyo to the earth mixture.

4. Place the stone into the bowl with the other ingredients.

5. Salute your spirits.

6. Take a mouthful of rum and spray the ingredients of the bowl.

7. Light a cigar and blow smoke directly onto the ingredients.

8. Using the ritual sacrifice prayer, sacrifice the rooster and the pigeon.

9. Pour the blood over the mixture and the stone.

10. Place the candles around the bowl.

11. Light the candles in honor of the spirits.

12. Allow the stone and the other ingredients to feed on the blood for 24 hours.

13. After the 24 hours, take all of the ingredients and place it into the hollow horn.

14. Seal the amulet with cement or a strong rubber glue.

15. Place the Cowries shell in the middle of the glue along with the seven different colored beads.

16. When the glue or cement has hardened, it is ready for usage.

This amulet should be kept in your pocket or purse. This amulet can be fed when you are feeding your spirits. The spirit of this amulet likes rum and cigar offerings. Do this about once a week to keep the spirit in your favor.

COLLARES OF PALO MAYOMBE

Collares refers to the beautiful beaded necklaces that are worn in the Santeria religion. Each necklace or collar has a different meaning and it's own set of powers.

In Palo Mayombe, the collares are used to control and to have great command over the spirits. Three of the most popular collares are the Collares De Egun, Collares De Bandera and the Collares De Los Guerreros. These three sets of collares when prepared in the proper ritual will produce incredible results. All of the Collares of Palo Mayombe can be consecrated when you are feeding your spirit.

COLLARES DE EGUN

The Collares De Egun represent our ancestors and our spiritual guides whom have been with us since birth. Ancestors are family members who have died and are now kneeling at the foot of God. The requirements for an individual to become an ancestor is the following.

1. The person must have died at an old age.

2. The individual must have died of natural causes.

3. The individual must have had children.

The Collares De Egun are made with a variety of multi colored beads. There is no sequence or pattern to the beads. The Collares usually are about 12 inches in length. The Collares are worn for protection on a daily basis and when you are also conducting spiritual consultations. The Collares De Egun give an individual great power and protection. Many Paleros prepare and give the Collares De Egun to individual's who are involved with illegal activities for protection.

COLLARES DE LA BANDERA

The Collares De Bandera are used by a Palero to have command over the dark spirits. The Collares De Bandera consists of a 4 foot long string of multi colored beads, Cowrie shells and a chain. The Collares De Bandera are worn over the left shoulder and are considered to be very powerful. These beads can be worn when you are conducting your magic works. These are the traditional beads worn by a Palero.

COLLARES DE LOS GUERREROS

The Collares De Los Guerreros are made from a metal chain about 4 feet in length. The chain contains many miniature implements such as tools and knives. The Collares De Los Guerreros can be worn in Palo Mayombe ceremonies and rituals for supernatural power. These powerful collares are also worn over the left shoulder.

CANDLES AND FIRE

BLACK CANDLES

Black candles are used for black magic and for strong spells of harm and destruction. If you will be working in Palo Mayombe, you should light at least one black candle for the spirits twice a week. The candles should be offered on Tuesday's and Saturday's.

WHITE CANDLES

White candles are used to elevate spirits and for working with the light spirits of Palo Mayombe. Thursday's are a good day to offer the spirits white candles.

RED CANDLES

Red candles are used in Palo Mayombe spells of domination and to have victory over enemies. Red candles are also used in Palo Mayombe love spells.

CRUCIFIX CANDLES

Crucifix candles are used on spiritual altars for the Egun. Crucifix candles are also used during Misas.

RED - Love Spells.

BLACK - Spells of Divine Justice.

WHITE - Healing and spiritual protection.

GREEN - To open up the roads.

SEVEN AFRICAN POWERS

Seven African Powers candles are a combination of seven different colors of wax. The world of the spirits is dark, but spirits are seen by spiritualists as rays of color. The spirits are particularly fond of these candles. A seven day Seven African Powers Candle should always be lit in the Casa De Los Muertos. This candle brings blessings and supernatural powers from the spirits of Palo Mayombe.

SKULL CANDLES

Skull candles are used when working with the spirits of Palo Mayombe. These candles can be placed near the cauldron of the spirit for spiritual communication.

WHITE - For communicating with spirits of white light. This candle is also used to free an individual who is possessed with an unclean spirit.

BLACK - For communicating with spirits of darkness. This candle is also used in spells of destruction.

DEVIL CANDLE

Devil candles are used when working with the powers of the dark or fallen angels.

RED - For dominating an individual.

BLACK - For spells of destruction.

GENDER CANDLES MALE

Gender candles are used to make a man impotent or a woman infertile. These candles are also used to tie a lover down.

BLACK - Used to make a man impotent.

RED - Used to dominate or tie a man to you.

GENDER CANDLES FEMALE

RED - Used to make a woman infertile.

BLACK - Used to dominate or tie a woman to you.

IMAGE CANDLE MALE

Image candles are also used to dominate an individual. They are used in spells of harm as well as for love.

RED - Used to dominate a man.

BLACK - Used to cause or inflict harm.

IMAGE CANDLE FEMALE

RED - Used to dominate a woman.

BLACK - Used to cause or inflict harm.

THE SECRETS OF THE PALO

A Palero Priest is an expert herbalist. One of the greatest and most powerful tools that a Palero can use are palos. Palos are special tree branches that are used extensively in the practice of Palo Mayombe. These magical tree branches when used in the correct way will produce great supernatural power. Palos have also been used medically treat diseases and illness. The Palo Una De Gata has been used to treat cancer, Leukemia, HIV positive and AIDS patients with great success. The Palo Una De Gata is administer in the form of a tea. An organized and serious Palero will always have a wide variety of palos at hand. In time, as you become familiar with the Palo Mayombe religion, the names and the meanings of all the palos will become memorized.

PALO AMARGO
This palo is used for protection and to have victory over enemies. Tie three small palos together with red thread and keep in your pocket as an amulet.

PALO VENCE BATALLA
This palo is used in spells of destruction. Make a powder with this palo and sprinkle over your enemies picture. Light a black candle for 9 consecutive days.

PALO JINA
A Palero Priest will use this type of palo for spiritual protection or in magic amulets. Bury a piece of this palo near the entrance of your front door.

PALO NAMO
This palo is used to open up the roads of opportunity. Make a powder with this palo and sprinkle it in your path on a daily basis.

PALO DULCE
This palo is used in love spells or to dominate an individual. Write the name of the the individual 5 times on a piece of brown bag. Place the paper on a plate and sprinkle a powder made with this palo over it. Light a red candle for 5 consecutive days.

PALO HUESO
This palo is used in money and prosperity spells. Use in candle dressings with green candles.

PALO JABON
This palo is used in strong cleansings and protection spells. Make a powder with this palo, mix with olive oil and anoint your forehead before going to bed.

PALO GUASIMO

A Palero will use this type of palo to eliminate gossip or to tie down a person's tongue. Write your enemies name 9 times on a piece of brown paper bag. Place the paper on a black plate and sprinkle 9 pieces of this palo over the paper. Light a black candle for 9 consecutive days.

PALO MUERTO

A very strong palo used in death spells or to put an end to any situation. Wrap the individual's picture around a piece of this palo. Wrap with black thread. Place the bundle into your spiritual cauldron.

PALO ACEITUNO

This palo is used to command or dominate other people. Make a powder with this palo and sprinkle over the picture of the individual. Light a red candle for 7 consecutive days.

PALO RAMON

This palo will give a Palero the ability to command dark spirits in his magic spells. Drill a hole through a medium size piece of this palo and place on a necklace made with purple glass beads. Use this necklace when casting spells.

PALO UNA DE GATO

This palo is used to put a hex or bewitch an individual. Take 3 pieces of this palo and burn together with black dog and black cat fur. Pulverize and sprinkle near the individual's home.

PALO GUAYABA
This palo is used in spells of Divine Justice or revenge. Make a powder with this palo and use with a candle dressing. The candles should be red and burned for 7 consecutive days.

PALO PINO
This palo is used in spells of harm. Wrap 9 pieces of this palo with a photo of the individual in a black silk scarf. Bury over a grave of an individual who died a violent death.

PALO AMANSA GUAPO
This palo is used in domination and extremely strong love spells. Make a powder with this palo and sprinkle it in the individual's home or clothes.

PALO JOBOVAN
This famous palo is used in court spells or to free an individual from jail. Make a powder with this palo. Sprinkle over a photo of the individual. Light a red candle for 9 consecutive days before the court hearing.

PALO CANPECHE
This palo is used to reverse magic spells. Make a powder with this palo and use in a candle dressing. The candles should be white or any type of reverse candle.

PALO OJANCHO
This palo is used by a Palero to cause conflicts between people or to separate lovers. Burn a piece of this palo with black dog and black cat fur. Pulverize and sprinkle in the individual's home or over a photo. Light a black candle for 9 consecutive days.

PALO GUARAMO
This palo is used for protection and inside strong supernatural amulets. Carry this palo in your pocket.

PALO GUAMA
This palo is used to open the gates of hell or to the spirit plane. Make a staff with this palo and use when invoking the spirits. Cover the staff with red and black beads.

PALO COCUYO
This palo is used to control the forces of nature. Burn this palo as you would an incense during rituals.

PALO ESPUELA DE GALLO
This palo is used to shut a person's mouth. Baptize a black wax figure candle in the individual's name. Tie a piece of this palo around its mouth. Wrap the wax figure with black thread and place into your spiritual cauldron.

PALO SANTO

This palo is used to control an individual. Make a powder with this palo and sprinkle it over the photo of the individual. Light a red candle for 7 consecutive days.

PALO CAMITO

This palo is used to shut a person's eyes. Draw a set of eyes on a piece of brown paper bag. Write the individual's name 9 times across the eyes. Wrap a piece of black thread around this palo. Bury it over the grave of an individual who died of sickness.

PALO TOCINO

This palo is used to kill a witch. Bury 9 pieces of this palo in the individual's yard.

PALO MULATTO

This palo is used in strong witchcraft. Make a powder with this palo and use it in a candle dressing or in a combination with other spells.

PALO TORCIDO

This palo is used to change a person's luck for the worse. Write the individual's name on a piece of brown paper bag and wrap it around the palo. Wrap with black thread and place it into your spiritual cauldron.

PALO NEGRO
This palo is used to remove obstacles in a person's path. Make a powder with this palo and burn it with frankincense and Myrah incense.

PALO BOMBA
This palo is used in black magic spells to destroy the foundation of an individual. Write the individual's name 9 times on a brown paper bag. Wrap it around the palo with black thread. Place the bundle in a mason jar with urine and vinegar. Light a black candle for 9 consecutive days. On the 10th day throw the work into running fresh water.

PALO CABALLERO
This palo is used to reverse witchcraft. Boil 9 pieces of this palo and add the liquid to a spiritual bath. Take this bath for 9 consecutive days. Light a white candle.

PALO CAMBIA VOZ
This palo is used to change a person's opinion. Write the individual's name 4 times on a piece of brown paper bag. Write your name across their name 7 times. Place on a white plate and sprinkle with a powder made with this palo. Light a red candle for 7 consecutive days.

PALO CAJA
This palo is used to punish a witch. Boil this palo in holy water. Sprinkle the magical liquid in the individual's yard.

PALO CLAVO
This palo is used to remove a curse. Boil this palo and use the liquid as part of a spiritual bath. Take this bath for 9 consecutive days.

PALO JERINGA
This palo is used in love spells. Use this palo as the same way as Palo Amansa Guapo.

PALO DIABLO
This palo is used in black magic spells. Use this palo in the same way as Palo Bomba.

PALO MALAMBO
This very strong palo is used to multiply the forces of darkness.

PALO MORO
This palo is used to give an individual great luck attracting love. Carry a piece of this palo in your pocket.

PALO MANGA SAYAS
This palo is used to keep a marriage or love affair together. Wrap a picture of both individual's around this palo and wrap with red thread. Place it into a mason jar and fill with honey. Keep for an indefinite period of time.

PALO VEN A MI

To make an individual come to you. This palo can also be used in strong love spells to make a lover return. Write the individual's name 5 times on two pieces of brown paper bag. Write your name across their name 5 times. Place it into the bottom of a pair of the other individual's shoes. Place 5 pieces of this palo into each shoe. Bury the shoes in the ground facing your front door.

PALO JUSTICIA

This palo is used in powerful court spells or to free an individual from jail. Use the same way as Palo Jobovan.

PALO CAMBIA RUMBA

This palo is used to make an individual's luck turn for the worse. Write the individual's name 9 times on a piece of brown paper bag. Wrap the paper around the palo and tie with red and black thread. Place the bundle into your spiritual cauldron.

PALO ABRE CAMINO

This powerful palo is used to open up the roads to opportunity and success. Wrap a piece of this palo with red and black beads. Carry in your pocket.

PALO ESPANTA MUERTO
This palo is used to cleanse an individual from the evil eye and also for protection from evil spirits. Make a spiritual bath with this palo. The individual should take this bath for 9 consecutive days.

PALO ESPANTA POLICIA
This palo is used to protect an individual from legal problems and from getting caught by the police. Use in the same way as Palo Espanta Muerto.

SPELLS OF PALOS

The following spells require the preparation of the palo sticks. For the best results, aguas or extracts of the palos are also used. The following is how to prepare Agua De Palo.

PREPARATION

1. Take a large palo and cut it into thin pieces. The length should be about 6 to 10 inches in length.

2. Place the thin sticks into a large mason jar and add rain water, river water and Holy water.

3. Cover the mason jar tightly.

4. Label the jar with the name of the palo inside.

5. Light a 7 day Seven African Powers Candle and place it next to the jar.

6. Place the jar in a dark place for 7 days.

7. After the 7 days, the palos will be ready to use as well as the Agua De Palo.

TO PROTECT YOUR HOME FROM YOUR ENEMIES

INGREDIENTS

1. PALO AMARGO
2. BLACK ROOSTER
3. 12 PENNIES
4. RED CANDLE

PREPARATION

1. Remove four small pieces of Palo Amargo from the water.

2. Place the palos in an offering dish.

3. Take a black rooster and sever it's head.

4. Allow the blood to drip onto the Palo Amargo.

5. Light a red candle.

6. After the candle has finished, bury the Palo Amargo in each of the four corners of your house.

The Palo Amargo should be buried at 12:00 Midnight along with three pennies in each hole.

TO DESTROY AN ENEMY

INGREDIENTS

1. PALO VENCE BATALLA
2. BLACK SALT
3. URINE
4. MILK
5. PRECIPITADO BLANCO
6. VINEGAR
7. BLACK CANDLE

PREPARATION

1. Write your enemies name on a small piece of brown paper.

2. Place the paper with the name into a medium size dark colored jar.

3. Place 7 pieces of Palo Vence Batalla into the jar.

4. Add the urine, black salt, precipitado, milk and the vinegar to the jar.

5. Place the lid of the jar on tightly.

6. Bury the jar in the cemetery.

7. Light the candle where you buried the jar.

FOR PROTECTION IN THE STREETS

INGREDIENTS

1. AGUA DE PALO JINA
2. CASCARILLA
3. RED CANDLE

PREPARATION

1. Pour the Agua De Palo Jina into a small cup.

2. Add cascarilla to the liquid.

3. Mix together well.

4. Light the candle.

5. Allow the mixture to stand for 24 hours.

6. After the 24 hours, pour the mixture into a small dark glass vial.

Carry this water with you for protection. When you feel that danger is near, sprinkle a little in your path. This powerful water has saved the life of many people from accidents and from being the victims of crime.

TO OPEN UP THE ROADS OF OPPORTUNITY
AMULET

INGREDIENTS

1. PALO NAMO
2. HUESO DE MUERTO
3. STRING OF RED BEADS
4. SEVEN AFRICAN POWERS CANDLE

PREPARATION

1. Glue four pieces of Palo Namo around a thin long piece of Hueso De Muerto.

2. Glue and Wrap the string of red beads around the cauldron and the Hueso De Muerto.

3. Place the amulet on a small plate in front of the cauldron of the spirits.

4. Light the candle in honor of the dead.

Carry this amulet when you are looking for employment or for business opportunity. A very powerful rare and expensive amulet, but always works.

FOR WEALTH AND PROSPERITY

INGREDIENTS

1. PALO HUESO
2. 2 DOLLAR BILL
3. 7 DIFFERENT COLORS OF THREAD
4. PALO MAYOMBE SPIRITUAL OIL
5. SEVEN AFRICAN POWERS CANDLE
6. GREEN MOJO BAG

PREPARATION

1. Wrap a $2 dollar bill tightly around the Palo Hueso.

2. Completely cover the palo and the dollar with all of the different threads.

3. Place the bundle in a small glass.

4. Pour the Palo Mayombe Spiritual Oil over the bundle and allow it to absorb.

5. Light the candle.

6. Place the glass with the bundle with the spirits for 24 hours.

7. After the 24 hours place into green mojo bag.

TO ATTRACT LOVE

INGREDIENTS

1. PALO DULCE
2. PALO AMANSA GUAPO
3. 7 DAY RED CANDLE

PREPARATION

1. Cut the Palo Dulce and the Palo Amansa Guapo into small pieces.

2. Take a picture of the individual that you desire and write your complete name on the back of the photo.

3. Write the other individual's name criss crossing your name.

4. Place the photo in a small jar with the palos.

5. Add the river water to the jar.

6. Light the candle and place it next to the jar.

7. Cover tightly and place the jar directly into the pot of the spirits for an indefinite period of time.

TO TIE AN INDIVIDUAL'S TONGUE

INGREDIENTS

1. PALO GUASIMO
2. PALO MUERTO
3. BLACK WAX FIGURE
4. 7 SMALL BLACK CANDLES

PREPARATION

1. Carve the name of the person who is the object of this spell on the black wax figure.

2. Light the black candle while preparing this spell.

3. Take 3 slivers of the Palo Guasimo and pierce the mouth of the wax figure with it. Leave the palos in the mouth.

4. Take a large piece of the Palo Muerto and drive it through the heart of the wax figure.

5. Take the wax figure to the cemetery and hang it from a tree.

This person is sure to learn a lesson quick. This spell starts to work within 36 hours.

TO CAUSE A PERSON TO HAVE CONFLICTS

INGREDIENTS

1. PALO UNA DE GAT0
2. ONE SMALL FROG
3. BLACK CANDLE

PREPARATION

1. Write the person's name on a piece of brown paper bag.

2. Place the folded paper into the frog's mouth.

3. Place a small piece of Palo Una De Gato into the frogs mouth.

4. Sew the mouth of the frog shut.

5. Place the frog into a small jar.

6. Cover the jar tightly.

7. Bury the jar in the yard of the individual.

As the frog dies, the person will start to have serious financial, legal and health problems.

FOR DIVINE JUSTICE

INGREDIENTS

1. SANTERIA KOSHER ROCK SALT
2. ONE LIME
3. PALO GUAYABA
4. PRECIPITADO ROJO
5. HOLY WATER
6. 7 SMALL RED CANDLES

PREPARATION

1. Write the person's name on a small piece of brown paper that is the subject of this spell.

2. Cut a lime in half and place it into a clear drinking glass.

3. Place the paper with the name into the glass.

4. Add the Holy Water to the glass.

5. Mix the Precipitado Rojo into the liquid mixture.

6. Place seven small sticks of the Palo Guayaba into the glass.

7. Place a small plate over the top of the glass.

8. Flip the glass and the plate over. Do not allow the water to come out.

9. Place a red candle on top of the glass and light it.

10. Do this for a period of 7 days.

At the end of the 7 days you will start to see results. The person will not know what hit them. This spell should be done at night between the hours of 9 and 12 midnight.

TO MAKE A MAN IMPOTENT

INGREDIENTS

1. PALO MUERTO
2. PALO PINO
3. ONE BLACK MALE PENIS CANDLE
4. ROPE
5. DOMINATION OIL
6. BALSAMO INTRANQUILO OIL
7. AGUA DE UNA DE GAT0

PREPARATION

1. Carve the full name of the individual three times on the candle.

2. Attach 7 pieces of the Palo Muerto around the candle.

3. Attach 7 pieces of Palo Pino around the candle.

4. Completely wrap the candle with the rope.

5. Pour both oils over the tightly wrapped candle.

6. Place the candle in a large dark jar.

7. Fill the jar up to the top with Agua De Palo Una De Gato.

8. Take the jar to the cemetery.

9. Bury the jar over the grave of a male individual.

10. Light a black candle and place it in the middle of the place where you buried it.

The only known antidote for this spell is for the individual to have a series of spiritual cleansing ceremonies.

TO CONTROL THE FORCES OF NATURE

INGREDIENTS

1. PALO COCUYO
2. MAY RAIN WATER
3. AGUA DE PALO MALAMBO
4. HOLY WATER
5. SEVEN AFRICAN POWERS CANDLE

PREPARATION

1. Place several large pieces of Palo Cocuyo into an empty wine bottle.

2. Add the May Rain Water to the bottle.

3. Add the Holy Water to the bottle.

4. Add the Agua De Palo Malambo to the bottle.

5. Place the cork back into the bottle.

6. Light the Seven African Powers Candle.

7. Place the bottle next to the candle.

8. Allow to stand for 7 days.

9. At the end of the 7 days, place this bottle with your other Palo Mayombe supplies.

This water can be used before spells for extra power or for spells where it is necessary to control the forces of nature. This water can be used in the same way as Holy Water is used.

DIRTS OF PALO MAYOMBE

Because a Palero Priest works strictly with spirits of darkness and the earth, the earth is a very important part to magic rituals. Paleros use a variety of different types of dirt to accomplish powerful spells.

TIERRA DE LOS MUERTOS

Tierra De Los Muertos is by far the most famous of the dirts used by Paleros. Tierra De Los Muertos is a collection of cemetery dirt from seven different cemeteries. This powerful earth can be used in the preparation of spiritual cauldrons, amulets for spiritual communication and also in spells of harm. This is the correct procedure to collect cemetery dirt.

PROCEDURE

1. Before entering a cemetery, it is necessary to ask those spirits who reside at that location for permission.

2. Before entering the cemetery, place 3 pennies near the front gate to the cemetery.

3. Take a mouthful of rum and spray it to the ground.

4. Light a cigar and blow the smoke directly to the ground.

This is a signal to the spirits that you are on friendly terms with them. Usually they will grant you protection and safe passage while collecting or performing rites in the cemetery.

OTHER TYPES OF DIRT

EARTH FROM FOUR STREET CORNERS
Used in Santeria as well as in Palo Mayombe. This dirt is used in powerful amulets.

EARTH OF EL MONTE
Paleros believe that there exists many spirits in the mountains. This dirt is used in spiritual cauldrons as well as in amulets.

EARTH FROM THE FOREST
Used in spiritual cauldrons and in magic amulets.

EARTH FROM FOUR JAILS
This earth is used in strong court spells to free an individual from jail, amulets to protect an individual from the law and also in spiritual cauldrons.

EARTH FROM FOUR BANKS
This earth is used in strong money spells and also in spiritual cauldrons and powerful business amulets.

EARTH FROM AN INDIAN CEMETERY
This earth is used in spiritual cauldrons, amulets and also in spells which enlist the aide of powerful Indian warrior spirits. This soil is extremely rare and difficult to find.

POWDERS USED IN PALO MAYOMBE

POLVO DE LOS MUERTOS
This extremely powerful powder is used in spells of destruction as well as in powerful amulets. This powerful powder is made in a variety of different ways, although it is traditionally scraped from the bottom of the spiritual cauldron.

HUESO DE MUERTO
This is an extremely rare and difficult to find powder. This very powerful powder is used in magical amulets as well as in powerful magical works. This is the strongest powder used in Palo Mayombe. Polvo Hueso De Muerto is made from the bones of the deceased.

POLVO DE VENADO
This powder is used in court spells and in amulets of protection. Polvo De Venado is made from a deer horn that has been ritually sacrificed.

POLVO DE SAPO AFRICANO
This powerful powder is used in Central American black magic spells. This powder is never used for amulets and is extremely dangerous. The powder is made from the African Frog.

POLVO DE CULEBRA
This powder is used in spells of harm and destruction. This powder is made from venomous snakes.

POLVO DE ESCORPION
This is used in black magic spells from Latin America. The powder is made from powered scorpions.

POLVO DE ARANA DE CEMETERIO
Used in Voodoo and South American magic spells. This powder is extremely difficult to obtain. This powder is made from spiders found only in cemeteries.

As shown on the cover, this is an example of a correcly constructed cauldron of the spirit Zarabanda.

This spiritual doll sits in the lobby of **Botanica El Montenegro** watching all who enter and leave. The doll called La Madama was prepared by a Palero Priest and contains a powerful spirit.

This picture was taken in one of the temple rooms of **Botanica El Montenegro** after a Spiritual Misa and cleansing ceremony. Elements of both Roman Catholic and Indigenous Amazon Indian statues can be seen. This is a typical altar used in Afro-Caribbean and Afro-Brazilian Spiritualism.

The Ceiba tree is perhaps the strongest and most powerful of the palos used in Palo Mayombe. The Ceiba tree is called the spirit tree because a Palero can perform many rituals at the foot of this magical tree. This photo was taken of a Ceiba tree in front of a Casa De Los Espiritus.

This rare photo of the Montenego Family was taken in Rio De Janiero around 1924. The photo represents three generations of female Brazilian Spiritualists.

SIGNATURES OF THE SPIRITS

PALO MAYOMBE
&
QUIMBANDA

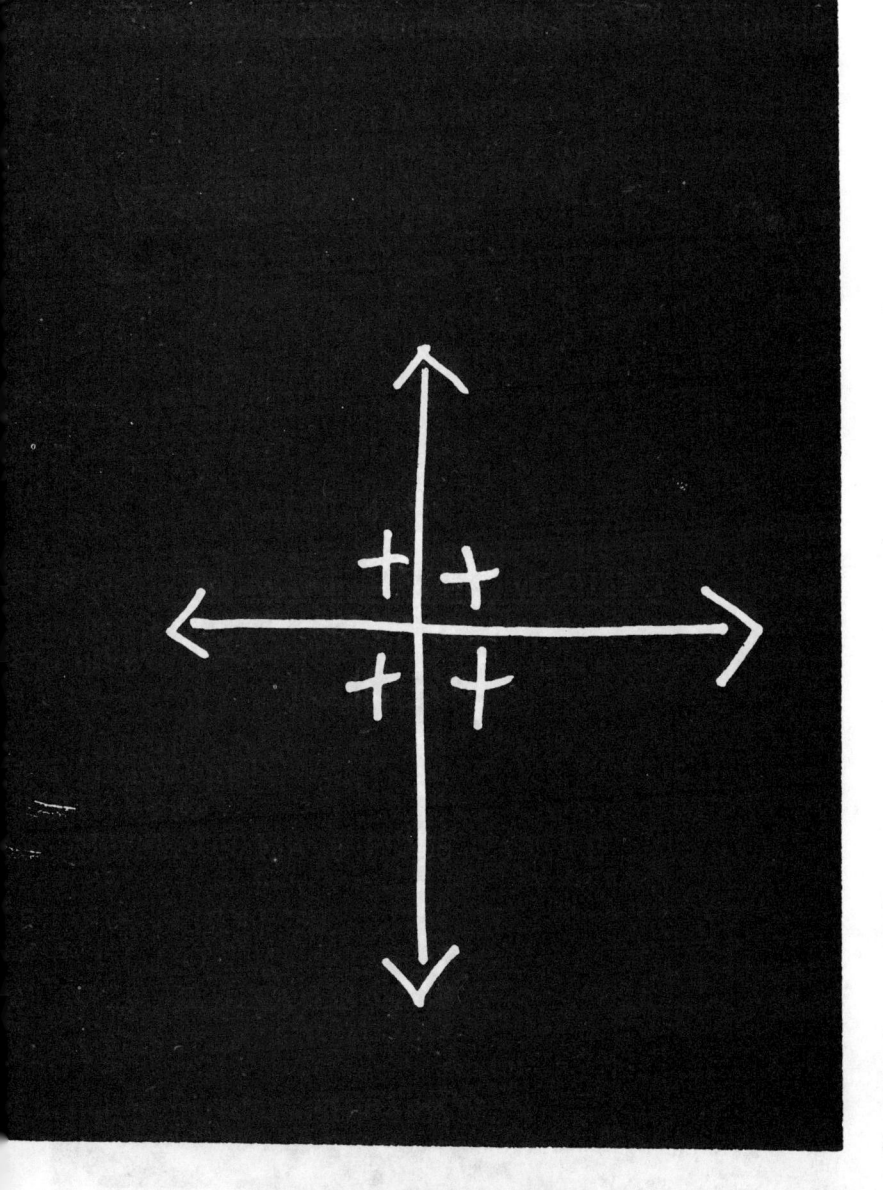

ZARABANDA

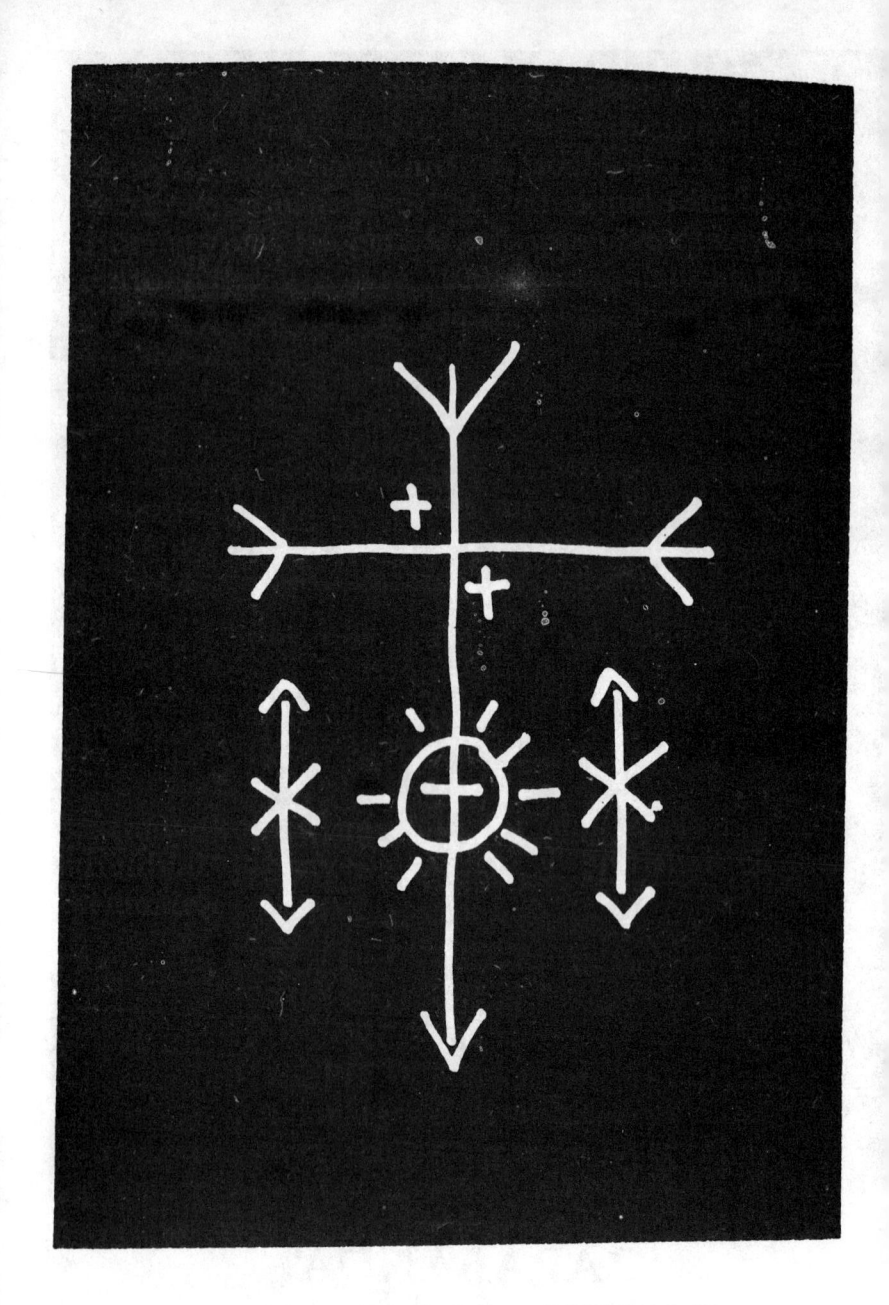

EL CRISTO NEGRO

EL CRISTO REY

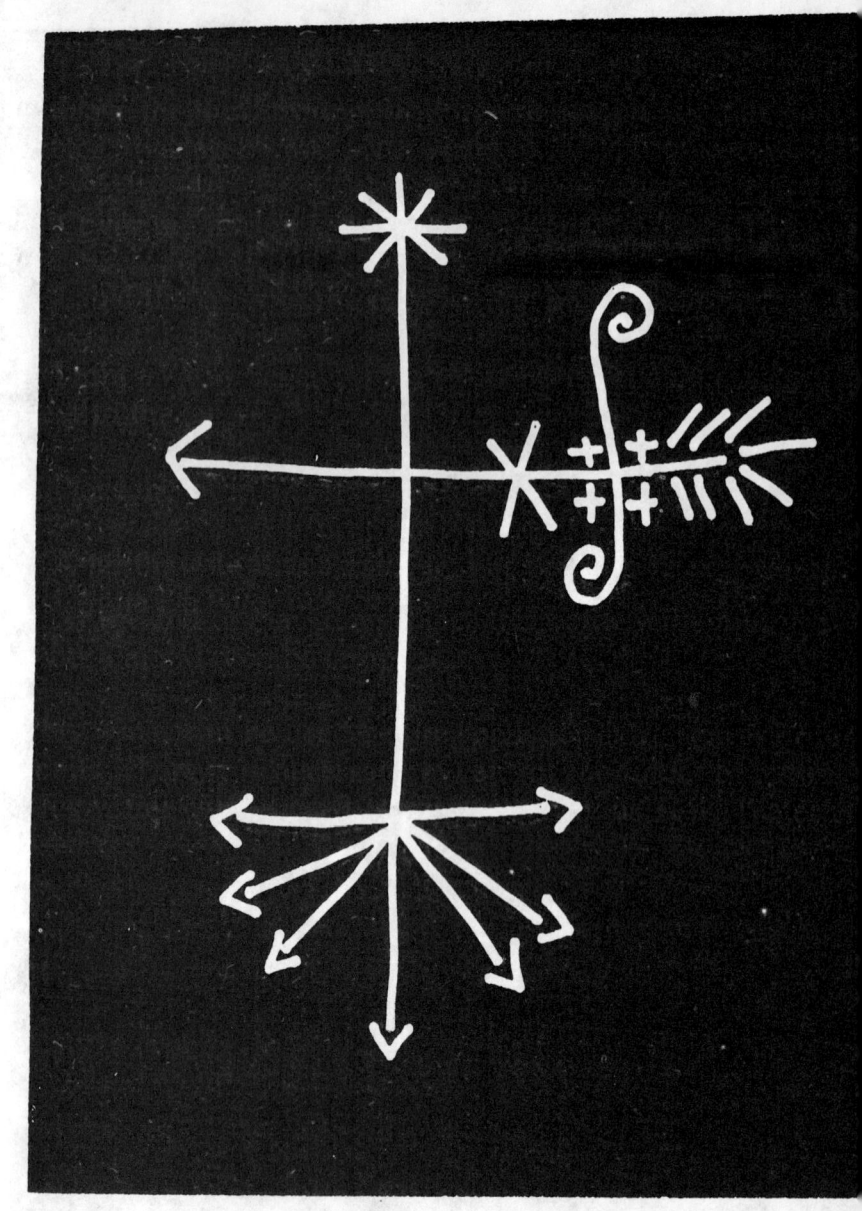

LOS ESPIRITUS INTRANQUILOS

MADRE DE AGUA

LA SANTISIMA PIEDRA IMAN

LA SANTISIMA MUERTE

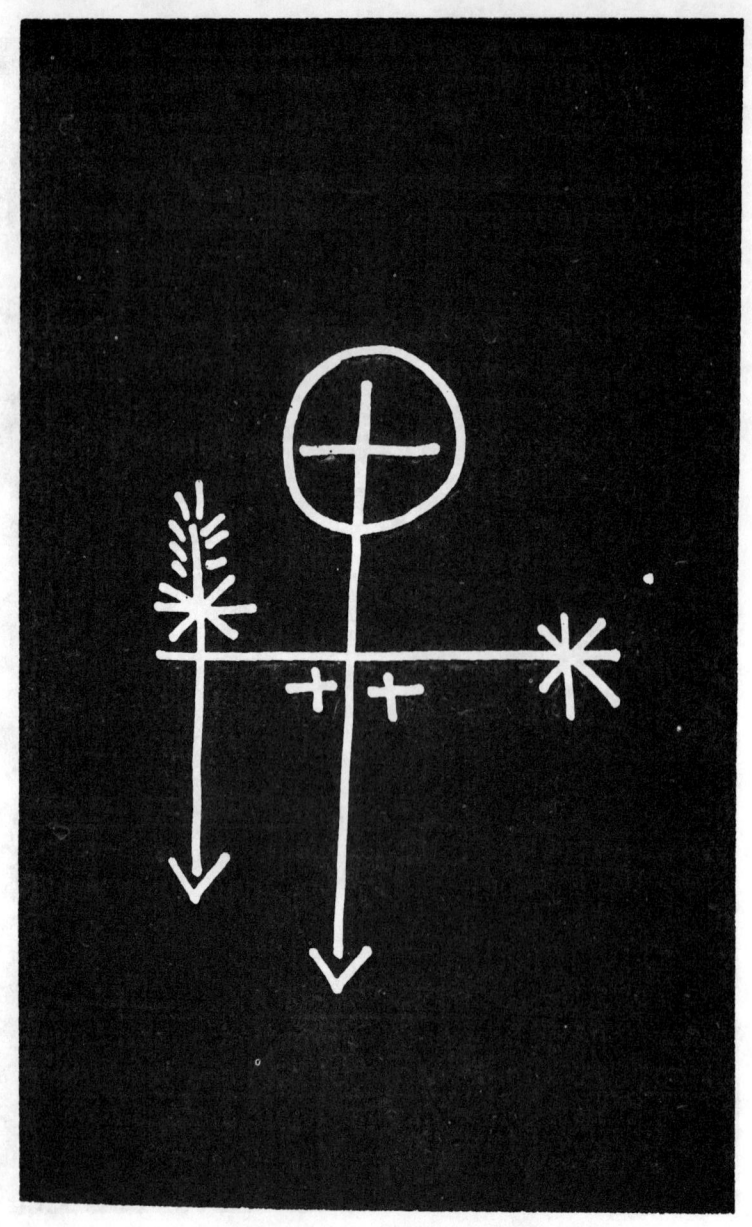

SAN SIMON

MADRE DE LA LUNA

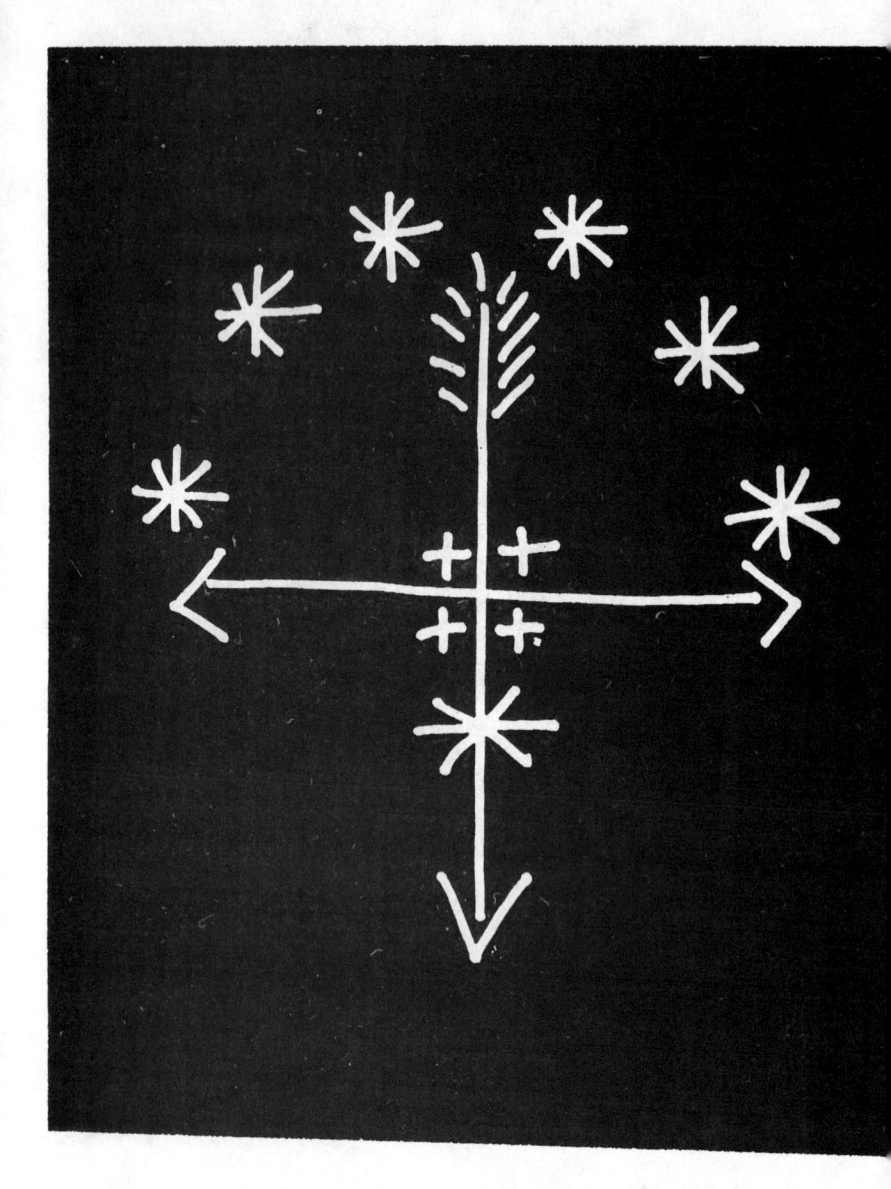

FRANCISCO DE SIETE RAYOS

MAMA CHOLA

BIBLIOGRAPHY

1. Cabrera, Lydia. <u>El Monte</u>. Miami, Florida: Ediciones Universal, 1992.

2. Garcia Cortez, Julio. <u>El Santo</u>. Miami, 1971.

3. Montenegro Miranda, Antonio. Interview. Los Angeles, California, 1994.

OTHER BOOKS BY CARLOS GALDIANO MONTENEGRO

POWERFUL AMULETS OF SANTERIA
This is a very rare book which explains the entire formulas and secrets for making 10 different paths of Eleggua. This book also contains formulas for making Ozains, Ochosi, powerful amulets for luck, love, money and protection.

SANTERIA - CANDLES, OILS, INCENSE, POWDERS
A MAGICAL GUIDE FOR SANTEROS AND PALEROS
This book will explain how to make traditional Santeria and Palo Mayombe oils, magical herbal candles, powerful incense and powders such as Polvo De Los Muertos, Black Salt and Polvo De Venado. This book also explains how to use these powerful ingredients in your magical spells for fast results.

MAGICAL HERBAL BATHS OF SANTERIA
Explore the mysteries of preparing magical herbal baths used in traditional Santeria and Latin American Spiritualism. This book contains lists of herbs, oils, powders and other magical ingredients used by Santeros for hundreds of years for preparing authentic Orisha baths, love baths, spiritual cleansing baths and a lot more.